CAPITAL & COUNTRY

THE FEDERATION YEARS 1900–1913

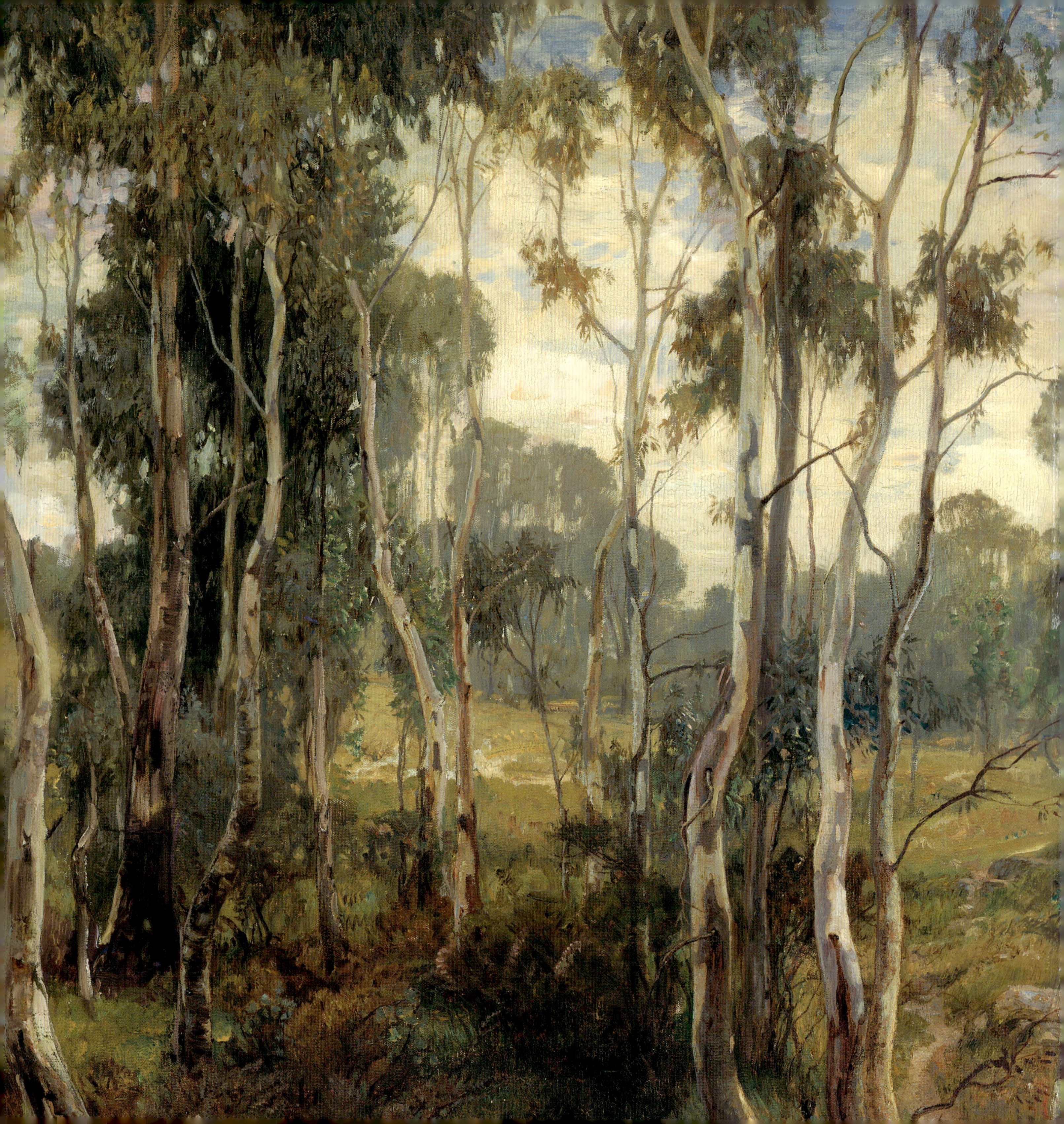

CAPITAL & COUNTRY

THE FEDERATION YEARS 1900–1913

Miriam Kelly

NGA NATIONAL GALLERY OF AUSTRALIA

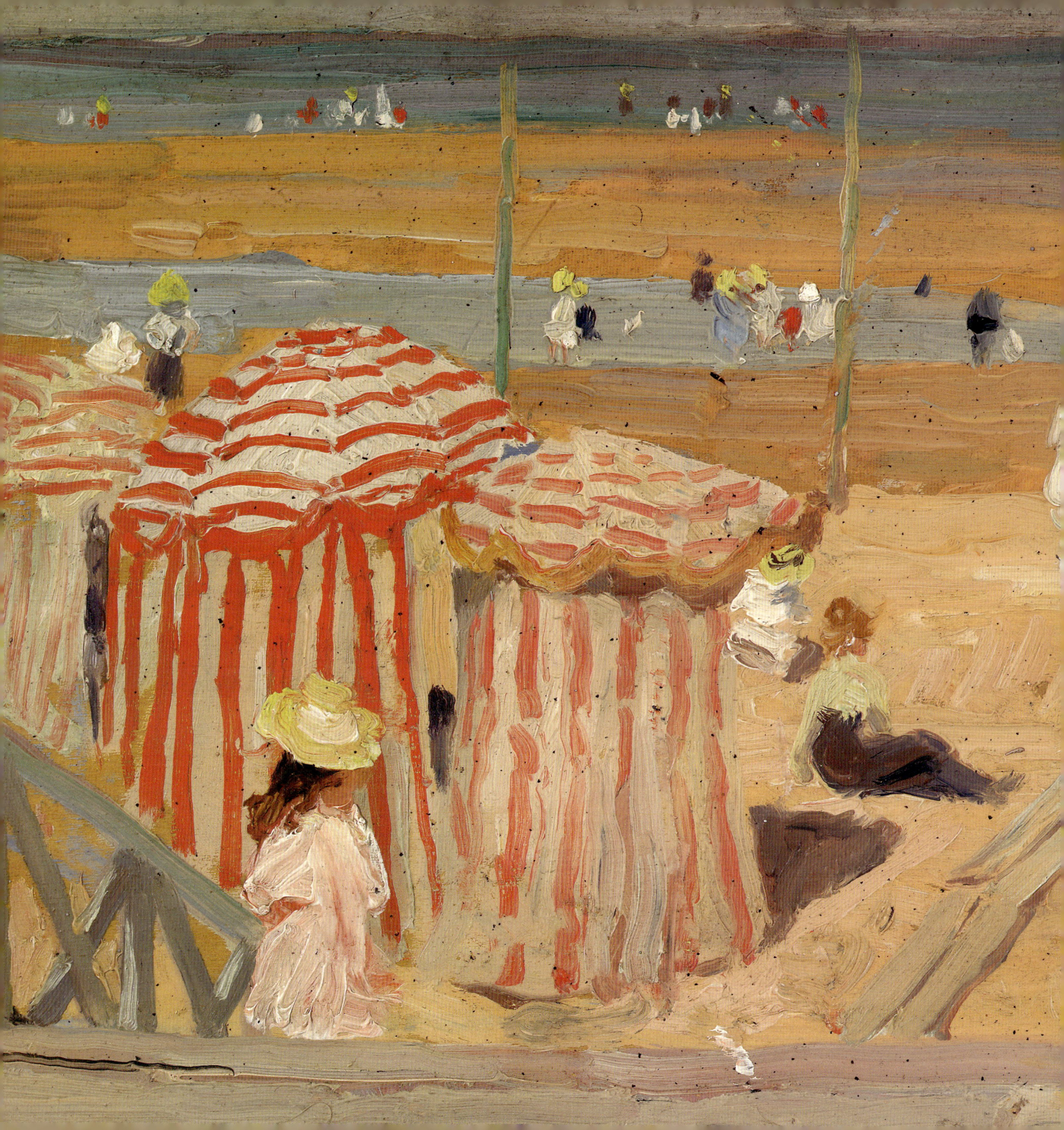

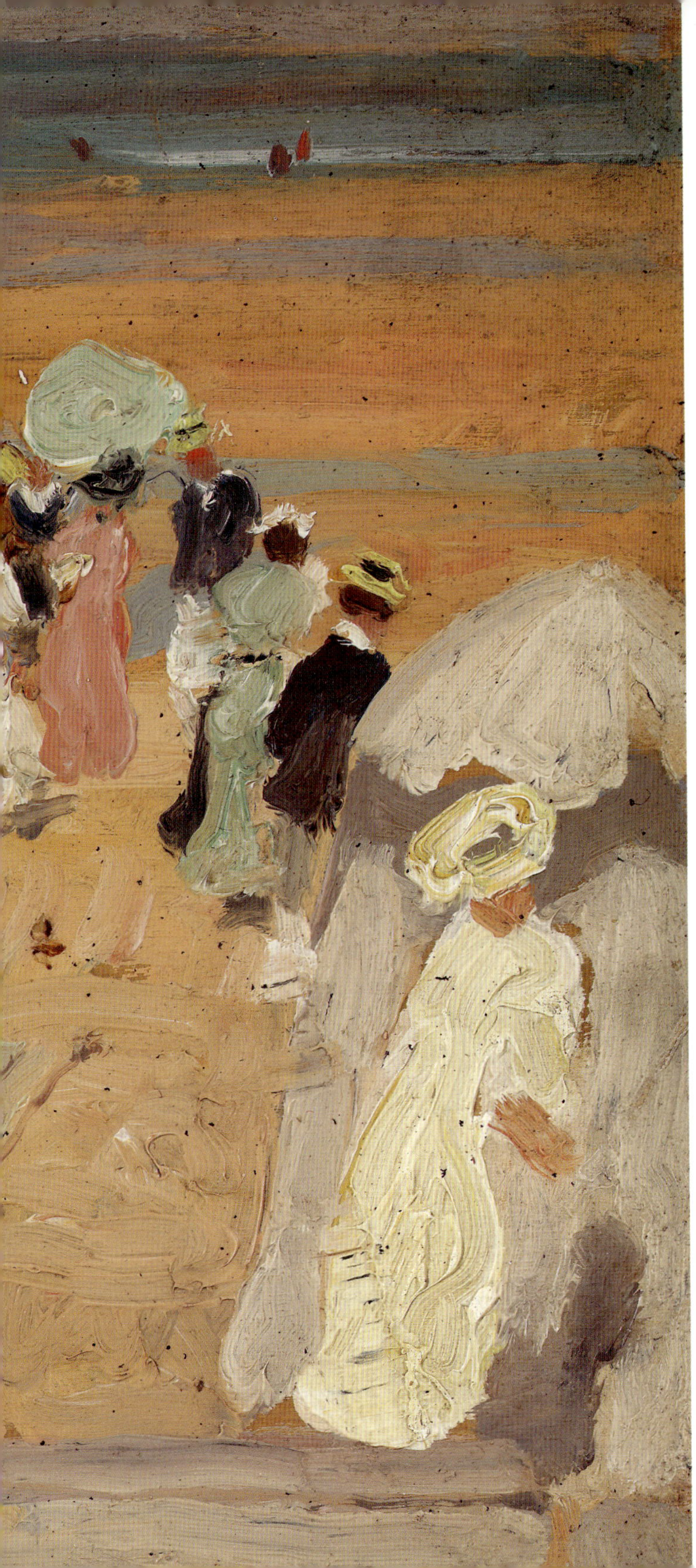

CONTENTS

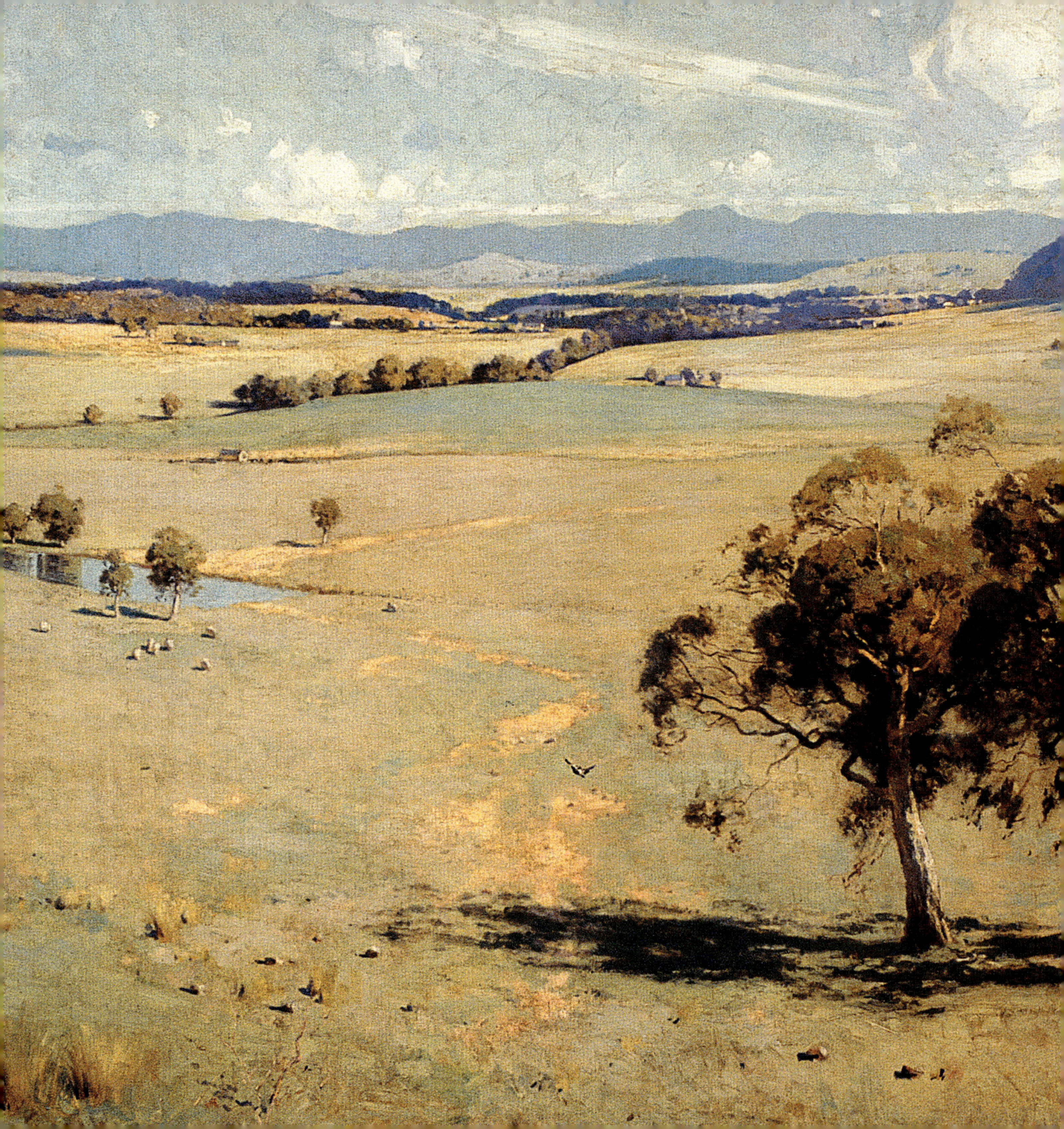

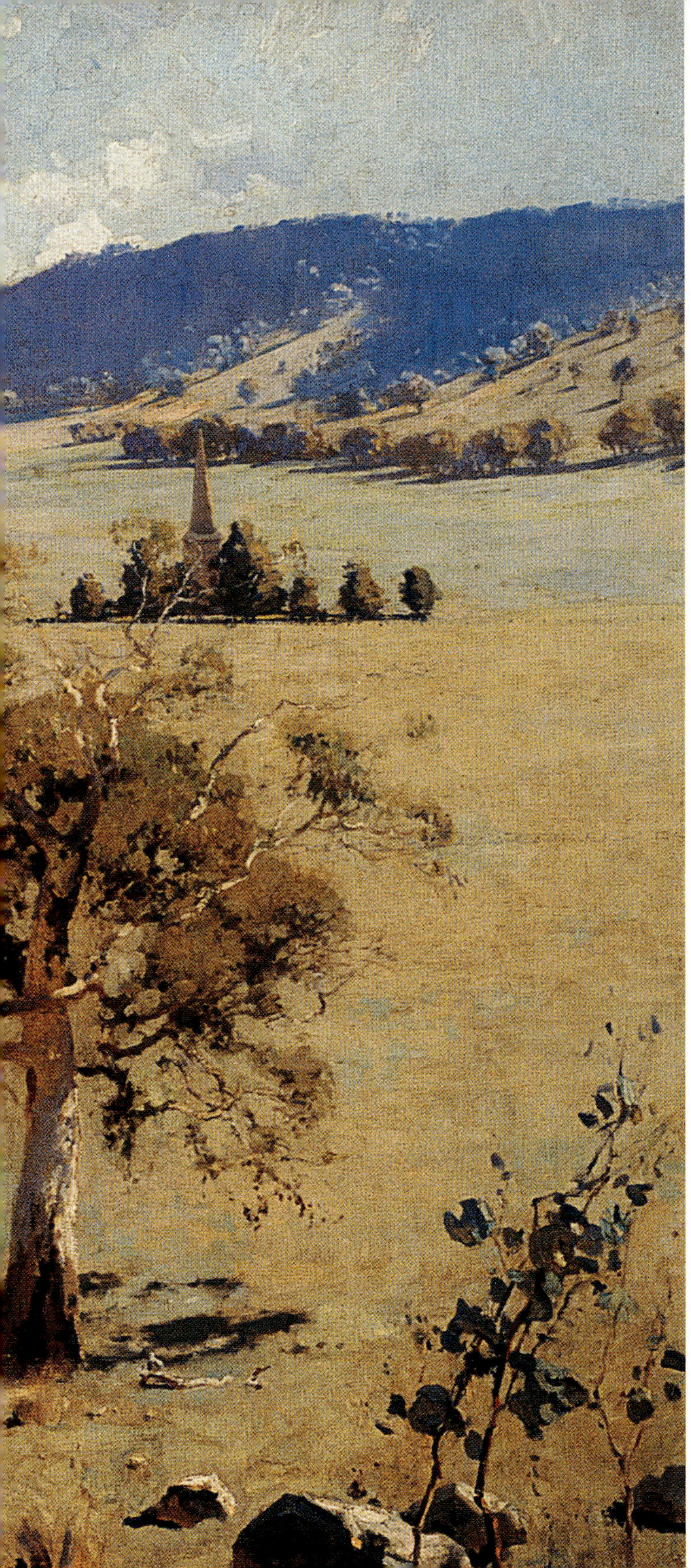

In 2013, Australia's national capital celebrates 100 years since the Foundation Stone for the city of Canberra was laid on Capital Hill, near where Australia's Parliament House now stands. The National Gallery of Australia, in Canberra, is celebrating the centenary with a gift to the nation of an exhibition, *Capital and country: the Federation years 1900–1913*, a touring show of major Australian paintings from the national art collection. This exhibition and the associated publication are also part of the National Gallery of Australia's ongoing exhibition program, which takes the national art collection to every state and territory around Australia.

Capital and country is the first major exhibition to consider the parallel stories of Federation landscape painting in Australia and the art produced by Australians who lived in Europe over this period from the turn of the twentieth century to just before the First World War. The pictures date from the Federation years 1900 to 1913 – known as the Edwardian era in Britain and the last years of the Belle Epoque in France – to the outbreak of the First World War in 1914. The selection of works brings to light the richness and diversity of Australian painting, ranging from images that convey the nation's enthusiastic and patriotic embrace of their own landscape, to those that emphasise the popularity of sophisticated portraiture and figure painting in Europe.

Well-known and loved paintings from the national art collection – scarcely off display in Canberra – are brought together with lesser-known works, including paintings recently acquired, conserved or appropriately reframed,

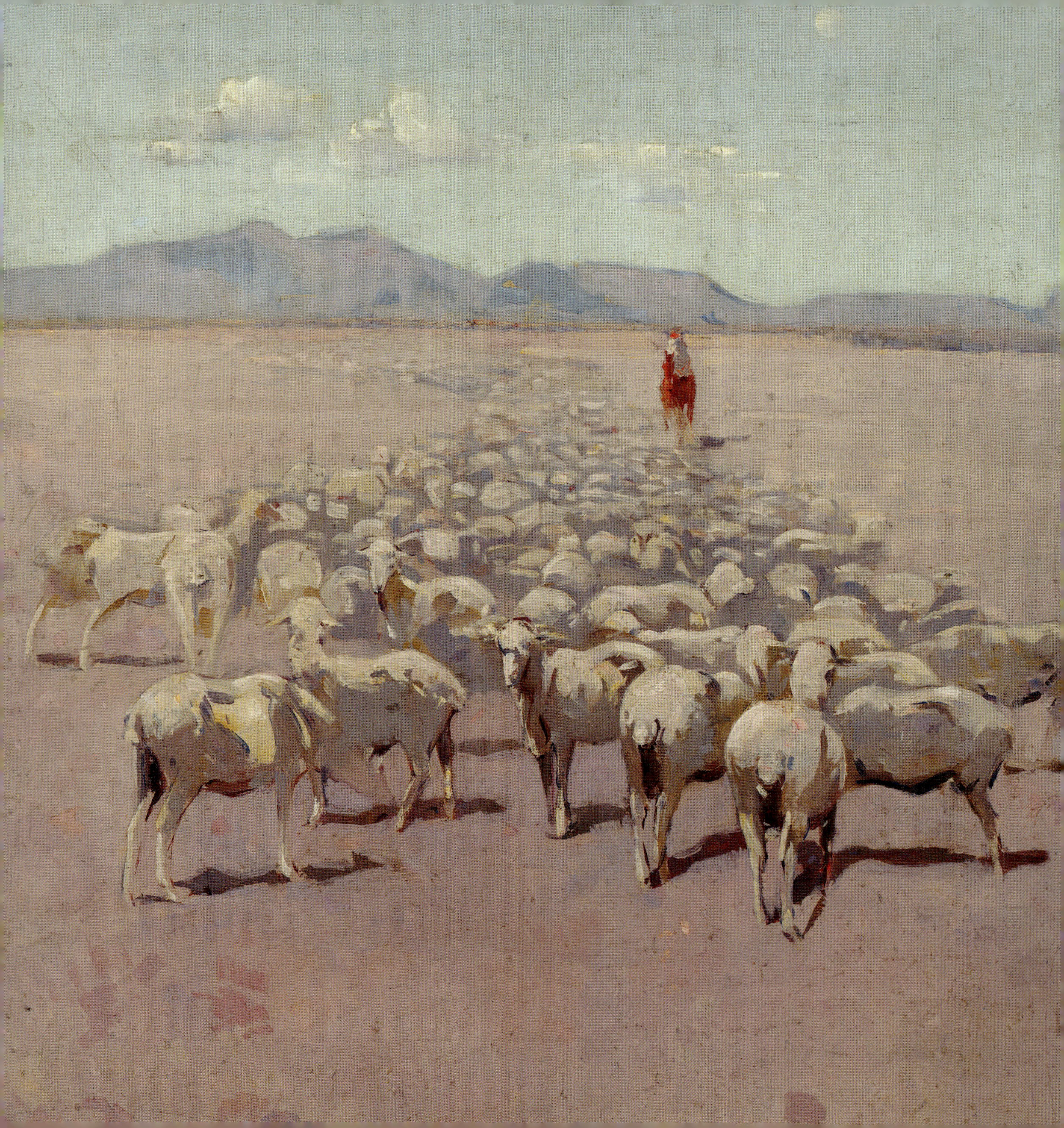

as well as works we have not been able to display at the
Gallery due to the limitations of space for our permanent
displays. All the works in this exhibition are in oil paint,
and while this era in Australia witnessed an enthusiastic
revival in watercolour painting, examples of these works
are not included in this touring exhibition, due to their
light sensitivity. Landscapes in watercolour became
immensely popular during this period – particularly
amongst private patrons – because they were works on
a domestic scale and were more affordable than oil
paintings. Artists such as Hans Heysen, Sydney Long,
J.J. Hilder and Blamire Young became well known for
their atmospheric use of watercolour.

W.C. Piguenit, Frederick McCubbin, Arthur Streeton
and Sydney Long are celebrated as some of the first
Australian-born artists to paint landscapes in this country.
An enthusiastic nationalist sentiment embraced their
Federation-period landscape paintings, as well as those
by Hans Heysen, W. Lister Lister, Penleigh Boyd,
Florence Fuller, Elioth Gruner and lesser-known artists
such as Harry Garlick and Frederick Leist.

In parallel, during this period major Australian painters
left Australia seeking 'the experience' of Europe and the
seal of approval of the 'Old World'. Established Australian
painters in the centres of Paris and London –Tom Roberts,
Rupert Bunny, E. Phillips Fox and Arthur Streeton – were
joined by a younger generation of artists including Max
Meldrum, George W. Lambert and Hugh Ramsay.

The exhibition has been curated by Miriam Kelly, Assistant
Curator, Australian Paintings and Sculpture. In her essay
she discusses key aspects of this era through the paintings
and stories of Australian artists at home and abroad. We
thank her for her diligent work which has brought the
period to life.

The Gallery is also grateful to the National Collecting
Institutions Touring and Outreach Program, and Visions
Australia, an Australian Government program that
supports touring exhibitions, for funding this exhibition.
The exhibition is also assisted by the Gallery's Council
Exhibitions Fund, which is made up of private donations
from Council members. We also extend our thanks to
the Australian Parliament House Art Collection and the
National Library of Australia, for their generous loans to
this exhibition.

We are delighted to be taking this major exhibition of
Federation-period pastoral landscape and expatriate figure
paintings to regional audiences around Australia to help
celebrate Canberra's Centenary year.

Ron Radford AM
Director

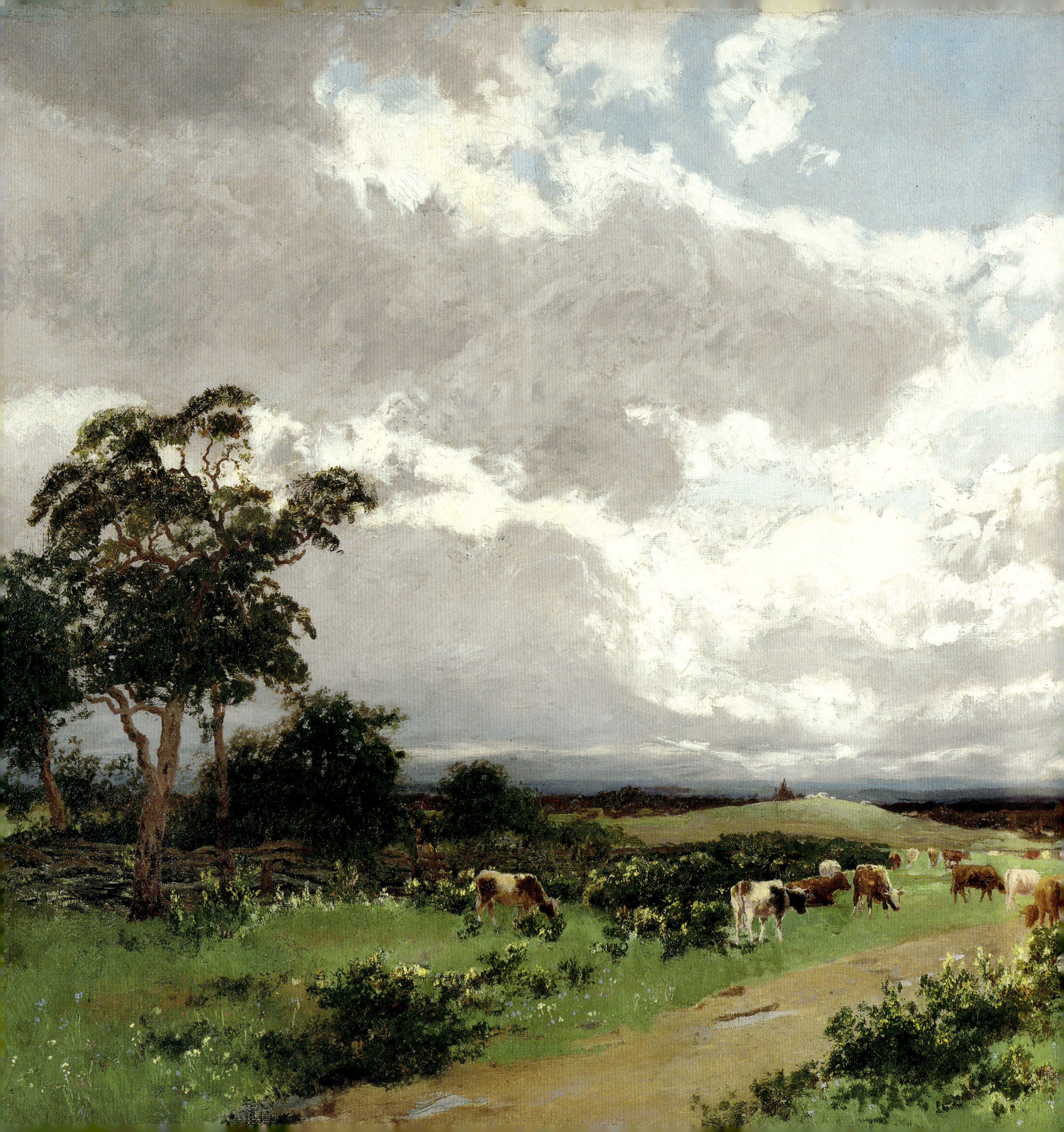

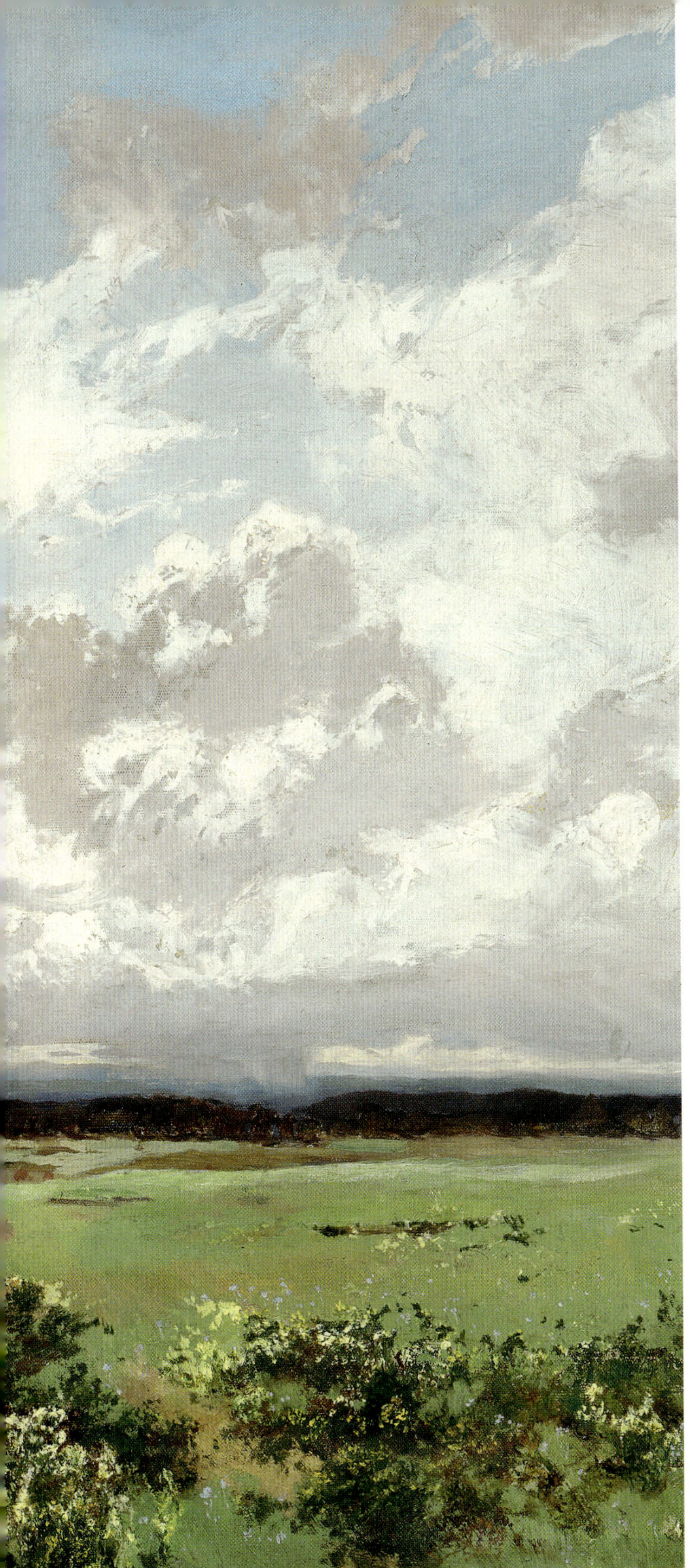

Changing perceptions 1913–2013

One summer night in Paris in 1901, the acrid scent of a gum leaf set alight by two young Australian painters in a small Montparnasse studio triggered nostalgic recollections of the Australian bush. In the twenty-first century, pictures of gum trees and the smell of eucalyptus still prompt imaginings of Australia. However, much has changed in the world we now inhabit and our ideas about the Australian landscape and our way of life are markedly different from those that ushered in the dawn of the federated nation.

What follows is a discussion of major paintings produced by Australian artists at home and abroad during a formative period of twentieth-century Australian history, between 1900 and 1913 – the Federation years. The selection of works in this exhibition range from shimmering stands of gum trees painted in the Australian bush, to grand figure compositions conceived in the bohemian enclaves of London and Paris. They are all painted by first or second-generation Australians.

Looking back from a global, multicultural Australia in the twenty-first century, it can be difficult to see these paintings within the context of their time – a period before two world wars, accelerating environmental degradation and significant reassessments of Indigenous and non-Indigenous cultural relations.[1] *Capital and country: the Federation years 1900–1913* seeks to encourage an appreciation of the paintings as works of art in the spirit in which they were made. Among Australia's predominantly European settler population, the Federation years were concurrently a time of national fervour and continuing reverence for the cultural centres of Europe.

A year of firsts

Never was a moonlit midnight in Sydney marked by a wilder, more prolonged, or generally more discordant welcome than was December 31, 1900 … the tumultuous uproar of the streets, where whistles, bells, gongs and accordions, rattles and clanging culinary utensils yielded unearthly sounds … Never on this side of the world was a New Year so freighted with expectations. It was actually, in a sense, the birthday of a whole people …[2]
Alfred Deakin, *Morning Post*, London, 8 January 1901

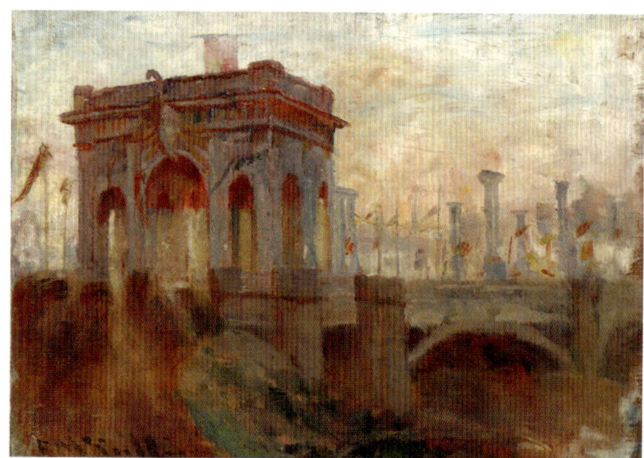

Frederick McCubbin
Triumphal Arch at Princes Bridge, Melbourne 1901
oil on pine panel, 26 x 34.4 cm
National Gallery of Australia, Canberra, given by Hugh McCubbin to the Commonwealth as a first-hand record of a great historical event and to mark the centenary of the birth of Frederick McCubbin, 1955

1901 was a year of firsts. On New Year's day the citizens of six colonies awoke as the people of a federated nation. Following more than a decade of resistance and debate, Federation was announced in Centennial Park, Sydney, by the inaugural Prime Minister, Edmund Barton and the Governor-General, Lord Hopetoun. The first Federal election was held in March. Two months later the inaugural Federal Parliament opened in the temporary capital of Melbourne, sparking a week of celebrations. Large crowds gave an enthusiastic welcome to the Duke of Cornwall and York (later King George V), who visited Australia for this event. By September, the Australian flag (which had earlier been selected from thousands of designs), flew proudly from the Exhibition Building in Melbourne's Carlton Gardens.

How did Australian artists respond to the moment of Federation?

Frederick McCubbin, among the first generation of locally born and trained painters, was keen to explore ideas of nationhood. He depicted the Federation parade through the city of Melbourne with exhilaration and a patriotic vision. Painted on-the-spot, *Triumphal Arch at Princes Bridge, Melbourne* 1901 conveys the infectious public jubilation, complete with fluttering standards and theatrical illumination. The arch on Princes Bridge was one of several especially constructed to mark the Duke and Duchess's journey to the Exhibition Building, where the official opening of Australia's first Parliament was held on 9 May.

Inside the Exhibition Building, Tom Roberts was poised on the balcony with anticipation. Having climbed to this elevated position with his wife Lillie, he 'was able to see that immense gathering of people from all over Australia, and from so many parts of the world'.[3] He wrote to his son that he was moved by the experience, describing it as 'very solemn and great'.[4] In his *Sketch for 'Opening*

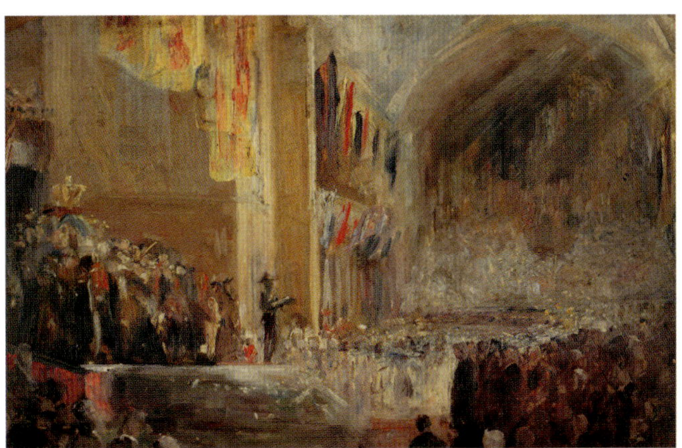

Tom Roberts
Sketch for 'Opening of Federal Parliament', 1901 1901
oil on academy board, 30.3 x 45.6 cm
National Library of Australia, Canberra

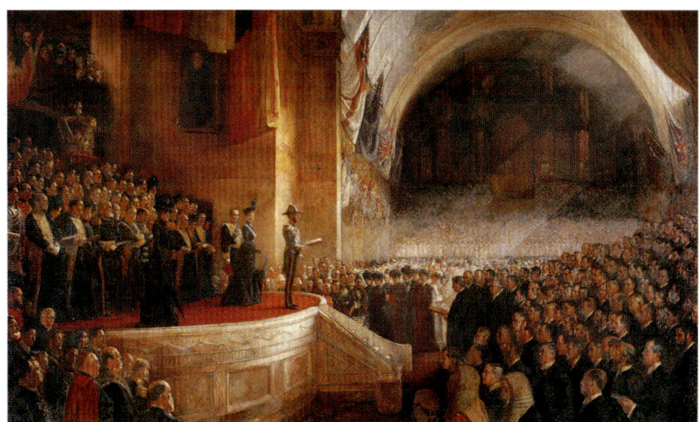

Tom Roberts
*Opening of the First Parliament of the Commonwealth of Australia by
H.R.H. The Duke of Cornwall and York (later King George V), May 9, 1901* 1903
oil on canvas, 304.5 x 509.2 cm
On permanent loan to the Parliament of Australia from the British Royal Collection
Photograph: Bruce Moore

of Federal Parliament', 1901 1901, Roberts captured an impression of the Duke in his royal regalia at the moment of his formal initiation of the Parliament. Roberts reserved touches of colour for the official party and the standards that flanked the stage, and deftly illustrated the scale of the crowd of thousands with contrasting tones of black and white.

In making this light-filled study, Roberts began what would become the most demanding commission of his career. Several days after the historic opening, he had been approached by a private organisation to paint the proceedings on a grand scale, with engravings after the painting to be produced and sold. A British and Australian-trained painter, Roberts had significantly contributed to Australian art in the lead-up to Federation with popular narrative paintings that celebrated both the landscape and the heroic qualities of rural working life.

To receive this major commission was a great honour for Roberts. In 1903, he wrote to Prime Minster Alfred Deakin of how proud he was 'to have put in my little bit to the Australian history'.[5]

However, by the time Roberts had completed over 250 individual portraits of politicians and dignitaries in the enormous final work, the delight of the small impression was lost. Measuring over three metres high and almost six metres wide, 'the big picture', also described as 'the big machine' by his friends, took Roberts almost two years to complete.[6] *Opening of the First Parliament of the Commonwealth of Australia by H.R.H. The Duke of Cornwall and York (later King George V), May 9, 1901* 1903, was presented to King Edward VII in London in 1903. Since 1988 it has been displayed in Australia's Parliament House in Canberra, on permanent loan from Her Majesty Queen Elizabeth II.

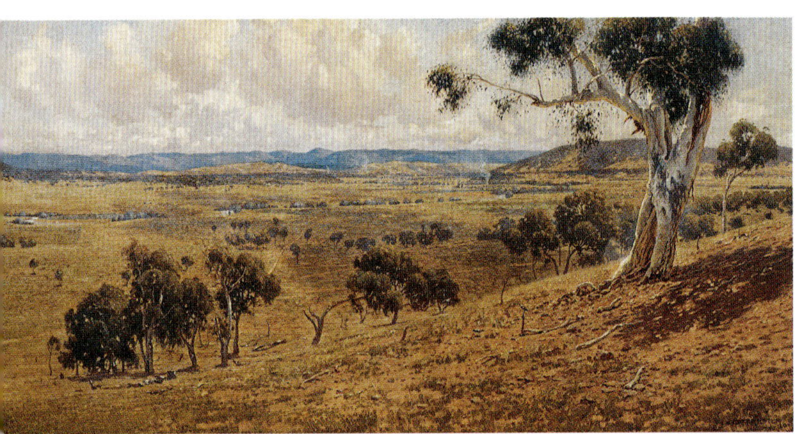

W. Lister Lister
Federal Capital site 1913
oil on canvas, 159 x 284 cm
Australian Parliament House, Canberra, Historic Memorials Collection, purchased 1913

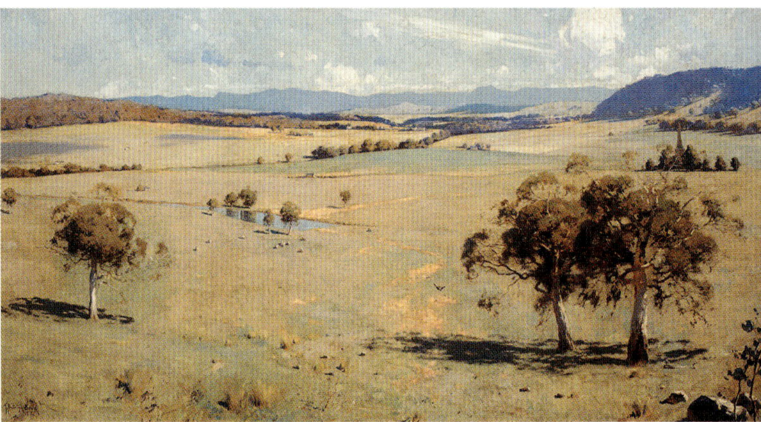

Penleigh Boyd
The Federal Capital site 1913
oil on canvas, 151 x 274 cm
Australian Parliament House, Canberra, Historic Memorials Collection, purchased 1913

New realities

The opening of Australia's Federal Parliament by the Duke of Cornwall and York heralded a positive continuing relationship with Britain, emphasising Australia's place as a nation still secure within the British Commonwealth.[7] Over the next thirteen years, the Australian Government asserted its increasing independence from the Crown and, among other initiatives, developed a defence department, established Australia's first international diplomatic presence in London and founded the Federal Capital.

The search for the site in which to locate the Federal Capital was played out amid considerable controversy for almost a decade following Federation. Possible locations were explored across New South Wales, from Bombala to Orange and from Hay to Tenterfield, following an agreement made in the 1890s by colonial rivals Victoria and New South Wales, that a site would be secured within New South Wales, but no closer than 200 kilometres to Sydney.[8] In 1908, the Federal Parliament finally agreed upon the Monaro plains near Yass.[9] In 1911, the experimental American architects Walter Burley and Marion Mahony Griffin won the commission to design the Federal Capital. Their visionary plan was inspired by the natural formations of the region and trends in urban planning, such as the Garden City movement.

To further promote the region proposed for the new Capital, in 1912 the Federal Government's Historic Memorials Committee established a competition to paint the Federal Capital site bathed in the bright clear sunlight of the 'midday effect' and with topographical accuracy.[10] W. Lister Lister and Penleigh Boyd painted grand, sun-drenched, golden vistas scattered with imposing gum trees, characteristic of many of the most successful Federation-era landscapes in their nationalistic subject matter, scale and palette. These images, simply titled the *Federal Capital site* and *The Federal Capital site* respectively, were awarded the acquisitive first and a surprise second prize in 1913.

The Federation landscape

Roberts anticipated the central role of landscape painting in the story of the new nation when he described the view over the crowd in the Exhibition Building in 1901 as being like 'a landscape stretching away'.[11] With the centenary of settlement in 1888, and with the approach to Federation, representations of Australia became increasingly nationalistic. Like Roberts, many artists throughout the 1890s helped to popularise history painting and created rural mythologies – of pioneers, bushrangers, women and children in the landscape, and bush life in general.

The nationalist concept of rural Australia that provided the Australian public with a sense of ownership and belonging into the Federation years excluded recognition of the layers of Aboriginal cultural history and relationship with the land; looking instead to the idea of an expansive, pastorally productive, heroic nation.

The ideals of home grown and Australian-made products gained currency in the marketplace during the Federation period. 'Billy Tea' and 'Cooee' branded products, like the virtues of Australian sunshine and wattle, were enthusiastically promoted and embraced.[12] Artist John Ford Paterson was one of a number of vocal exponents of a home-grown culture in the arts. In 1906 he encouraged Australian artists 'not [to] worry over much about getting a ticket to Paris or London, but to sit tight and paint'. He described their mission as 'to make people in love with their country, to show them its beauty and splendour, and thereby create a patriotic, a national sentiment'.[13]

Australians did indeed fall in love with their country. They actively sought out images of their nation that tapped into the desire for a distinctive identity, as well as ideals of an egalitarian way of life. Major Australian landscapes began to replace British works as favourites in state galleries.

From the 1890s and into the new century major public galleries in each state had been established, resettled or expanded, allowing for the display of many more works.[14] Public galleries in Brisbane and Perth were founded in the 1890s, while in Melbourne the National Gallery of Victoria was significantly expanded. In Sydney, the Art Gallery of New South Wales (known as the National Gallery of New South Wales well into the twentieth century) developed its first permanent display spaces in the Domain between 1896 and 1909. In Adelaide, the Art Gallery of South Australia (then National Gallery of South Australia) relocated in 1900 to the spacious historic building on North Terrace.

Public and private patronage reflected the enthusiasm for Australian landscapes as the country recovered from the financial crash of the 1890s, resulting in an art market boom by 1907.[15] The major bequests of Sir Thomas Elder to the Art Gallery of South Australia in 1898 and Alfred Felton to National Gallery of Victoria in 1904 made it possible for the galleries to acquire significant Australian works, as well as several important European paintings. The annual *Federal Art Exhibition* in Adelaide, established by the South Australian Artists' Association and the Art Gallery of South Australia in 1898, became a context for artists to present major works, with an eye to acquisition by Australia's public galleries.

Critics and artists keenly discussed the exhibition and acquisition of Australian landscapes, charting developments over the Federation era from the escalating size of works to the celebration of a warmer, often grey-green and gold palette, felt to be peculiar to this country, and indicative of an 'Australian character'.

Sunlight and eucalypts

'It represents a typical Australia scene', wrote one South
Australian reviewer about Hans Heysen's 1904 exhibition,
'blue gum saplings at the side of a creek, and the consonant
brown undergrowth – all telling of a characteristic fidelity
to nature on the part of the artist.'[16] In the early years of
the twentieth century, representations of the gum tree,
the effects of sunlight and bush life were enthusiastically
lauded as characteristic of the Australian landscape.
Heysen had recently returned to South Australia at the
end of 1903, after almost four years abroad, studying in
the ateliers of Paris and painting *en plein air*.

Heysen was struck afresh by the quality of Australian
sunlight. He immediately immersed himself in the
landscape of the Adelaide Hills where he observed sunlight
effects. In *The saplings* 1904, a subtle morning glow
envelops a stand of young eucalypts. 'It always appears to
me', Heysen wrote in 1912, 'that Australia has a *something*
individual in its light that colours local substances.'[17] The
new light of morning, along with the fading romance of
the end-of-day, had captivated landscape painters from the
late nineteenth century into the early Federation years.
However, by around 1908 atmospheric light effects were
outmoded by the popularity of the strong, clear, Australian
midday sun.[18] Heysen later stated that while in Europe 'you
look at scenery through a veil of atmosphere; in Australia
you so often look straight through to the scene without
anything interposing between you and it. Clarity of light
is like a religion to us in Australia.'[19]

Heysen's *The saplings* also anticipates his most significant
contribution to Australian painting. He realistically
painted the slender, sinuous forms of the eucalypts with the
utmost attention to details of texture and colour; rendering
the individual curls and cracks in the bark and the many
tonal variations within the trunks. In the works he painted
after 1908, Heysen depicted the heroic, gnarled trunks

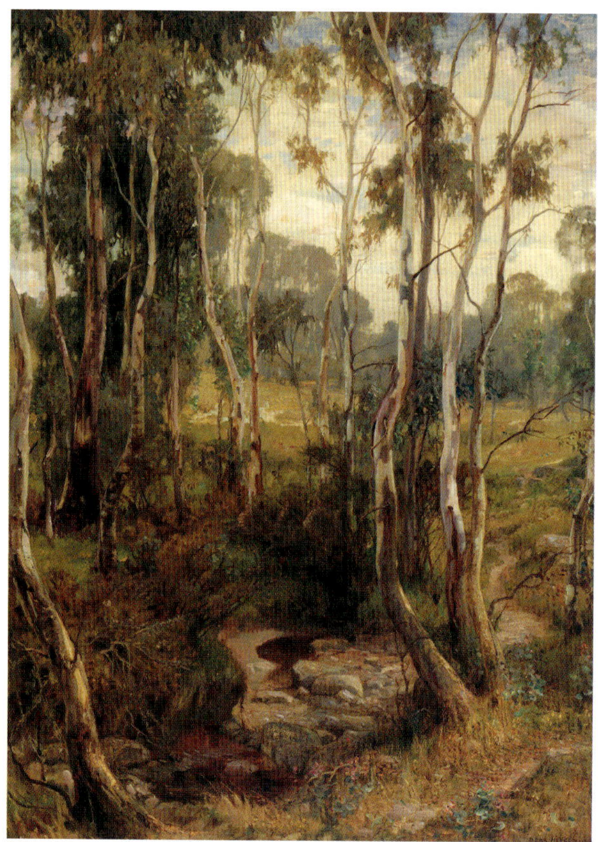

Hans Heysen
The saplings 1904
oil on canvas, 120.5 x 90.3 cm
National Gallery of Australia, Canberra, bequest of Millie Hay Joyner 1993

of mature river red gums, helping to elevate the gum tree
as a symbol of Australia.[20] Inherent in his celebration
of the gum tree, as in the works of a number of his
contemporaries, was Heysen's concern for the increasing
deforestation of the land, which he witnessed around his
bush home near Hahndorf in the Adelaide Hills.

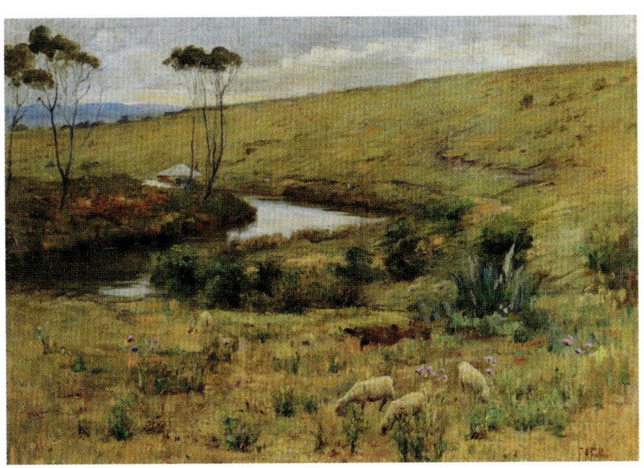

Florence Fuller
Dawn landscape c. 1905
oil on canvas, 44.5 x 60 cm
National Gallery of Australia, Canberra, purchased 2011

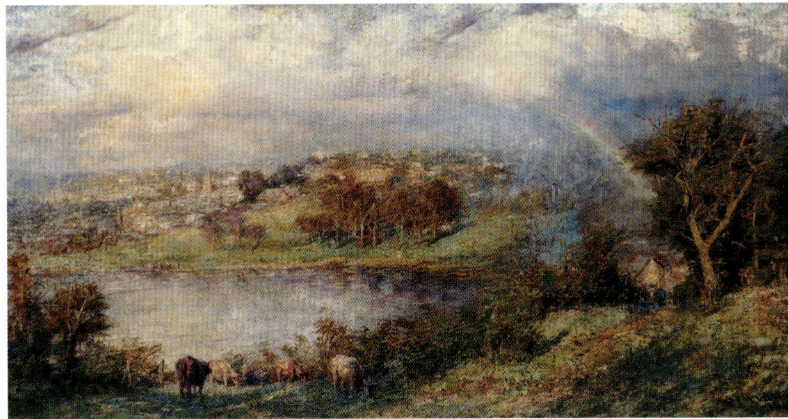

Frederick McCubbin
Flood waters 1913
oil on canvas, 92.5 x 182 cm
National Gallery of Australia, Canberra, purchased 1973

Celebrating the bush

Throughout his career, Frederick McCubbin spent extended periods in the bush, on the outskirts of Melbourne.[21] In 1901 he established a home and rural retreat for his family at Mount Macedon, where he painted at weekends. His understanding of the bush and great affection for his surroundings are evoked in his most sophisticated and personal paintings of the Federation era. By 1909 he was described as possessing the very 'scent of the eucalyptus in his being'.[22]

McCubbin was well into his fifties before he was able to make a long desired pilgrimage to Europe to view major works of art. He was particularly moved by the Romantic landscapes of J.M.W. Turner and John Constable, as well as the work of Claude Monet.[23] Seeing these works encouraged him to become more adventurous in his approach to colour and handling of paint. He wrote to Tom Roberts that 'in our past work we have been too timid'.[24]

McCubbin returned to Australia at the end of 1907 and saw the landscape afresh, in hues akin to the Australian opal. In place of the grey-green palette that had dominated his earlier work, he celebrated 'the varieties in shades and colours the gum tree presented'.[25] His revitalised vision is seen in works such as *Flood waters* 1913. With its rainbow arching over the swollen banks of the Yarra River, this lyrical late work was praised at the time for creating an atmospheric sense of place.[26]

A 'national school' of painting

Despite the profound influences of his six-months abroad, like Paterson, McCubbin advocated that 'the Australian artist can best fulfil his highest destiny by remaining in his own country and studying that which lies about him …' and felt that 'an art is national in so far as it sympathises with the life and the beauty of the country it belongs to'.[27]

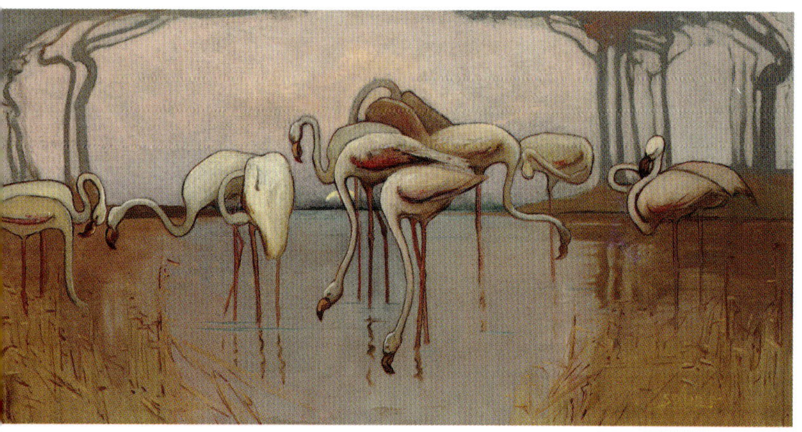

Sydney Long
Flamingoes c. 1907
oil on canvas, 30.6 x 61 cm
National Gallery of Australia, Canberra, acquired with the assistance of the Masterpieces for the Nation Fund 2006

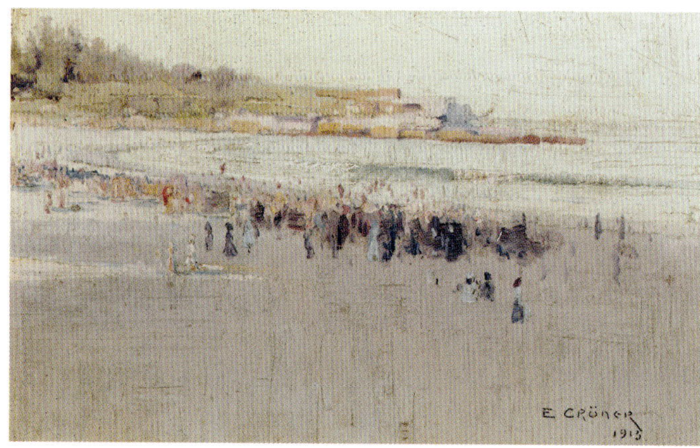

Elioth Gruner
Figures at Coogee 1913
oil on wood panel, 14.9 x 23.3 cm
National Gallery of Australia, Canberra, purchased 2009

McCubbin and Paterson were two of the many artists who contributed to the vigorous debate about what might characterise a 'national school' of painting, as well as the perceived necessity of a European training; ideas that had divided commentators and artists around the country since the late 1800s. The Queensland painter Godfrey Rivers, in an article in 1898, had warned of the necessity for a 'close and intelligent observation of nature … to express ourselves more in harmony with our natural surroundings' rather than 'hampered by traditions which have grown up under other skies.'[28]

Sydney Long advocated in an article for a national art that would convey the poetry in the 'lonely and primitive feeling of this country'.[29] His landscapes of the era have a sense of spiritual presence, at times expressing an awareness of the significance of an Aboriginal Australian relationship with the land. However, Long drew on the decorative European influences of Art Nouveau and

Symbolism to express this spirituality. He exaggerated the sinuous and elegant forms of tall, slender eucalypts in his aesthetic responses to the light and colour and mood of the bush, particularly at early evening. In his highly stylised composition *Flamingoes* c. 1907, the moon rises in a pink sky, while the silhouetted trunks of gums are echoed in the graceful shapes and vibrant natural hue of a flock of non-native birds.

In the same article of 1905, Long complained about the ubiquity of the rural worker in Australian painting: 'the drover, the shearer, the bullock driver, and even the bushranger … seem to be all that is needed as a keynote for Australian landscape'.[30] Like the gum tree, the itinerant worker had become symbolic of Australia. One such character is featured in Harry Garlick's sparse image *The drover* 1906, yet the subject of this painting is the parched Australian landscape, the pastoral colours bleached by the sharp heat of the bright Australian sun. Garlick painted

The drover in response to the devastation of what became known as the Federation drought, spanning the years 1895 to 1903.[31] In this context Garlick's rural worker presents an idealised masculine heroism, a strong yet quiet resilience in the face of hardship.

The ideal of an Australian bush worker was predominantly masculine in the Federation era, just as the characteristic bohemian artist was male. The majority of the students who trained in Australia's art schools from the late nineteenth century were women, yet only a small number of strong women painters came to the fore. A number of the artists' societies that had emerged in the 1880s were initially exclusive to men, and the major scholarships to study abroad were similarly not open to women until later in the twentieth century. Women supported and encouraged by family, such as Florence Fuller, were able to dedicate their lives to their art and fund their own travel and training abroad. Returning from Paris in 1904, Fuller lived and worked in Perth for four years until 1908. She painted impressions of Western Australian life and landscape, particularly rural vistas depicting the Western Australian flora. *Dawn landscape* c. 1905 captures a characteristic poetic quietude.

Towards modern Australia

Up until the founding of the Federal Capital, all Australia's capital cities and other major centres were developed along the coastline. Representations of urban life at the beach had been popular since the 1880s and, during the Federation period, public sea-bathing in daylight was legalised and popularised, with the first lifesaving clubs established to cope with numerous enthusiastic Australians who could not yet swim.[32] During the Federation era, images of the beach – such as the bustling, gem-like composition of clothed and bathing figures in Elioth Gruner's *Figures at Coogee* 1913 – reflected modern aspects of life.

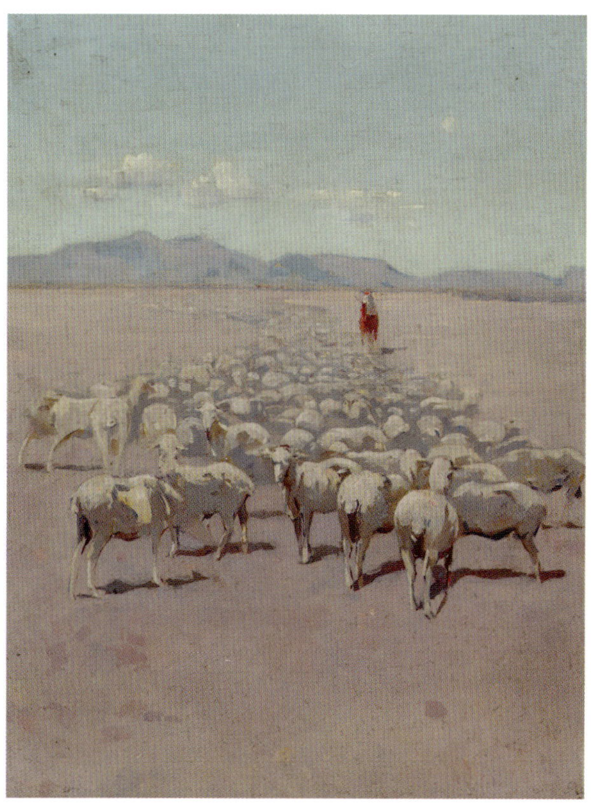

Harry Garlick
The drover 1906
oil on canvas board, 60.8 x 45.4 cm
National Gallery of Australia, Canberra, purchased 1972

The year 1914 marks the end of what can be called the Federation era. With the outbreak of the First World War, the jubilant creativity of the new century was cut short by the scale of Australia's sacrifice. The stories of Federation landscape painting were set aside in later histories of Australian art. Instead, the period between 1900 to 1913 was characterised as one of expatriation.[33]

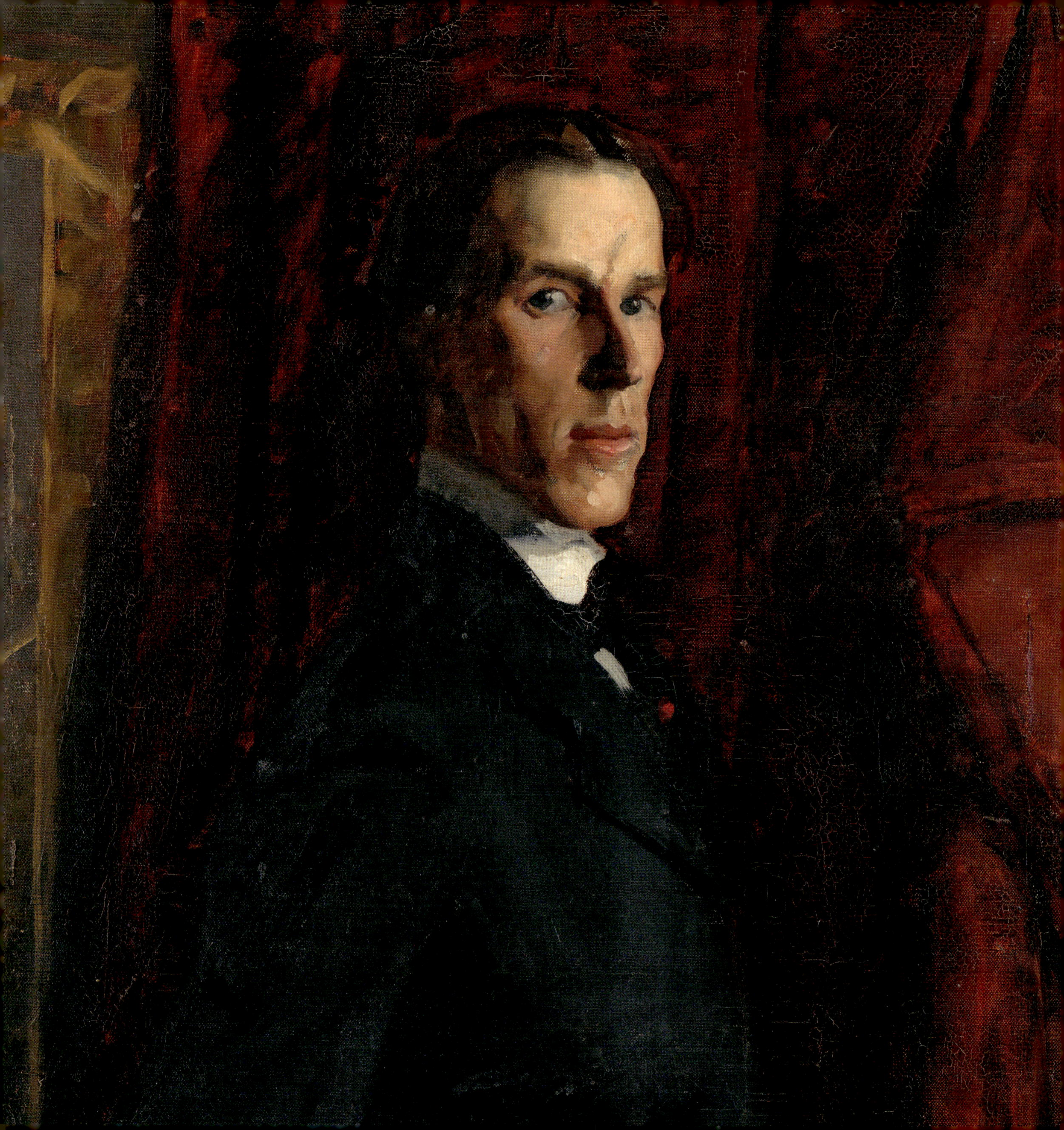

Paris and London

A pilgrimage to Europe in the Federation era was considered a rite of passage for many Australian artists. Teachers, patrons and colleagues encouraged promising young artists to study abroad and to see important works of European art. From the mid 1890s, major travelling scholarships in Sydney and Melbourne provided added impetus and some financial support for further study in the ateliers in Paris. In 1899, Max Meldrum was awarded the National Gallery of Victoria Travelling Scholarship and George W. Lambert received the New South Wales Travelling Scholarship. By the turn of the century, emerging artists and senior painters, such as E. Phillips Fox and Arthur Streeton, had also sought an escape from a dwindling Australian market for art during the 1890s depression.

For Hugh Ramsay, travelling abroad to study and seek further exposure had always been a matter of when and how, but never 'if'. At the age of 23 years, Ramsay sailed for Europe with meagre savings.[34] His elegantly penned letters home to Melbourne during three years abroad brim with hopes for success in Paris and London, and about the art that inspired him. 'It is a revelation to see all the grand works of the Old Masters' he enthused during his first Parisian winter, in 1901:

> Each is so perfect in its own way, that it makes you feel a
> veritable baby … but somehow there is a stimulating
> influence as well … Velasquez for ideal realism, Rembrandt
> for colour and realism, Correggio for grace, Titian for colour,
> also Veronese and Tintoretto, Van Dyke for refinement and
> poetry of line, Raphael for graceful line, Michelangelo for
> grandeur of design … They just open your eyes in fine style
> and broaden your ideas.[35]

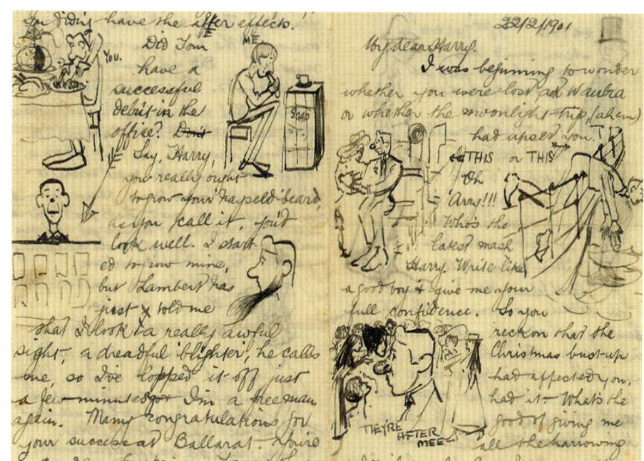

Hugh Ramsay to Harry Ramsay, 22 February 1901
Ramsay letter archive, IRN184368
National Gallery of Australia, Canberra

These letters are also interspersed with witty observations and illustrations of his daily life, from moonlight serenades by Parisian cats and attempts to grow a bohemian beard, to the more serious trials of homesickness and poverty. The realities of making ends meet was a challenge shared by all expatriates at times, particularly in their early years abroad. By living in close proximity within enclaves in Paris and London, most expatriate students and emerging artists jollied each other through the hardships – Ramsay even hired a piano for his small studio, 'so we keep the cats awake at night', and to encourage impromptu musical soirées of artists, writers and musicians.[36]

Figure painting and portraiture

At this time, London and Paris were the most fashionable centres of European art, attracting artists from all over the world. The era between 1900 and the First World War

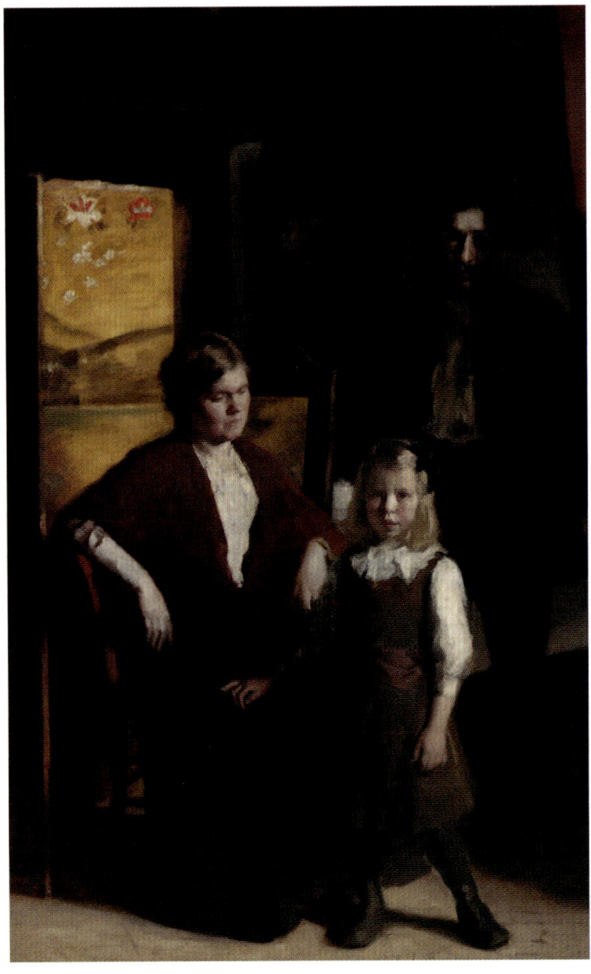

Max Meldrum
The yellow screen (Family group) 1910–11
oil on canvas mounted on composition board, 217.5 x 140 cm
National Gallery of Australia, Canberra, purchased 1969

(page 20)
Hugh Ramsay (detail)
Self-portrait c. 1902
oil on canvas, 45.8 x 40.4 cm
National Gallery of Australia, Canberra, purchased 1965

encompassed the last heady years of the Belle Epoque in France, and the Edwardian era in Britain. The death of Queen Victoria in 1901 and crowning of the more liberal King Edward VII prompted a shift in values and ideas about art. The popularised 'Whistlerian' approach of 'art for art's sake' came to characterise the sumptuous surface qualities of finely executed and often intentionally subject-less figure compositions. This heralded a move away from the nineteenth-century Victorian academic values of imparting historical narratives and moral tales. Around the turn of the century, the subject of painting became painting itself. Figure compositions and portraiture dominated the art scene within which Ramsay and fellow expatriates sought acceptance. They most admired those artists who gained prominence in the large annual exhibitions, particularly at the Old and New Salons in Paris and the Royal Academy in London.

The refined figure compositions of American-born, London-based James Abbott McNeill Whistler, a key exponent of the Aesthetic movement of the 1880s and 1890s, provided inspiration well into the new century. '[It] doesn't seem to have been painted, but just thought on by a most refined and distinguished mind', wrote Ramsay in admiration of Whistler's application of paint.[37] As students in Paris, Ramsay and George W. Lambert experimented with the surface qualities of their paintings, influenced by Whistler's stylised compositions and tonal palette, as well as by the bravura brush work of London-based American painter John Singer Sargent. They also looked back in European art history to the brush work and compositions of European Old Masters, especially to seventeenth-century Spanish painter Diego Velázquez.

The allure of the past: European Old Masters

Ramsay's statement that the works of Old Masters opened his eyes could have been uttered by almost all expatriate among artists – no master was more admired in London and Paris – in part fuelled by British art critic R.A.M. Stevenson's 1896 reassessment of the artist's composition, colour, modelling, illusion and brush work within nineteenth-century aesthetic sensibilities.

In *The yellow screen* (*Family group*) 1910–11, Meldrum paid homage to Velázquez's most renowned painting, *Las meninas* (*The family of Philip V*) c. 1656 (Museo Nacional del Prado, Madrid) by painting himself into his family group. Meldrum had begun to explore his own theories of painting by 1910, based on a study of the realist tradition, referencing the figure compositions of Velázquez through to the rural landscapes of mid-nineteenth century Barbizon school painter, Camille Corot. 'The study of the Old Masters gave me courage to go and look at nature and study it first hand', Meldrum later reflected.[38] He established a practice of painting directly from life, with a rapid application of colours within a restricted tonal palette. A controversial figure owing to his fiery temper and apparently radical theories, on his return to Melbourne in 1913 Meldrum presented public lectures on these ideas. He then turned his attention to the Australian landscape and established a school of painting, where he influenced artists including Clarice Beckett and Percy Leason.

The vogue for sophisticated quotations from Old Master paintings delighted the European press. Reporters enthusiastically played guessing games and chased references for their readers.[39] Lambert, who had painted heroic images of bush life in Australia in the 1890s, focused almost entirely on figure painting in London. He referenced the art of the past to add resonance to his contemporary images, gleaning from the allegorical compositions of sixteenth and seventeenth-century Old Master works through to the settings and poses of British eighteenth-century 'grand manner' portraits, such as those by Joshua Reynolds and Thomas Gainsborough.

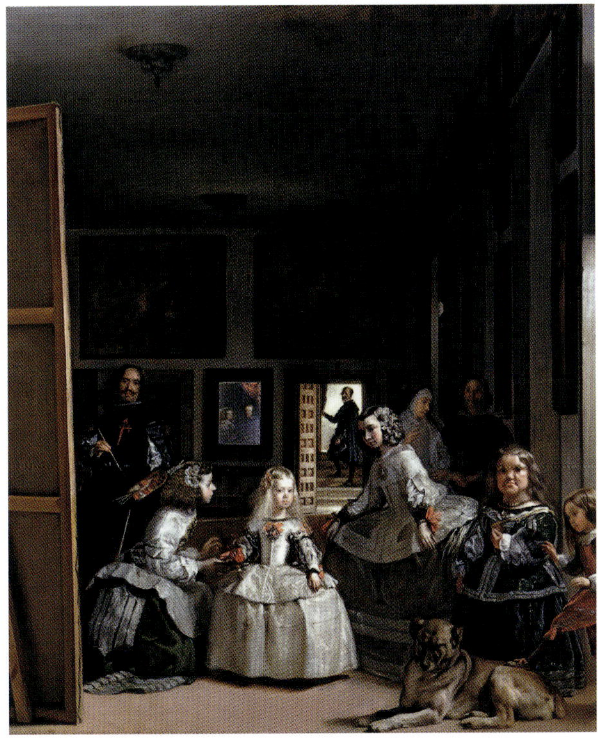

Diego Velázquez
Las meninas (*The family of Philip V*) c.1656
oil on canvas, 318 x 276 cm
Museo Nacional del Prado, Madrid
© Giraudon / The Bridgeman Art Library

Australian artists of the time. Max Meldrum was one of many painters who spent hours perched on a small stool in the galleries of the Musée du Louvre in Paris, making copies of major historical works in an attempt to discover the secrets of their success. (In fact, he spent more time in the galleries than in classes at the ateliers that he had travelled so far to attend.) The works of Velázquez in particular took hold of Meldrum's heart and brush. By this time Velázquez had achieved cult-like status

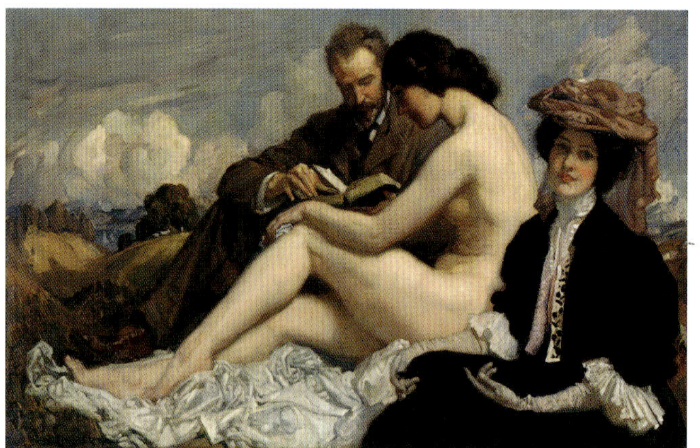

George W. Lambert
The sonnet c. 1907
oil on canvas, 113.3 x 177.4 cm
National Gallery of Australia, Canberra, bequest of John B. Pye 1963

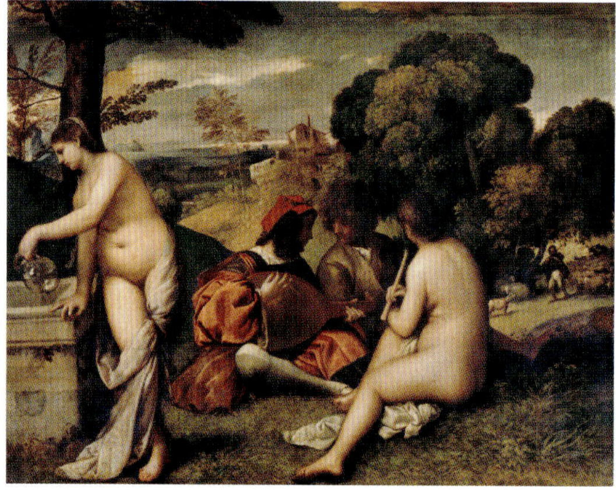

Titian
Le concert champêtre [*The pastoral concert*] c.1509
oil on canvas, 105 x 136 cm
Musée du Louvre, Paris
© RMN-Grand Palais (Musée du Louvre) / Hervé Lewandowski

The sonnet c. 1907 was the outcome of a scene Lambert observed in his studio one day when Australian artists Arthur Streeton and Thea Proctor and his regular nude model Kitty Powell were all momentarily in the same space. '[I]t seemed to me', he wrote, 'a modernized version of Giorgione's "Fete Champetre" [*sic*, now attributed to early Titian].'[40] The original *Le concert champêtre* [*The pastoral concert*] c. 1509 (Musée du Louvre, Paris) depicts two nude women conjured in the imagination of two young men by the magic of poetry and music. *The sonnet* reveals Lambert's delight in rendering the surface qualities of skin and cloth, as well as leaving his work open to a variety of possible interpretations by contemporary viewers.

For Lambert, like many of his contemporaries, commissioned portraiture was an essential part of maintaining a living and supporting a more experimental practice. E. Phillips Fox's portrait *Elsie, daughter of*

H.W. Brooks, Esquire 1904 was commissioned with the new wealth of an Australian industrialist, Henry Wilson Brooks, living in London with his family to further his Melbourne glass business.[41] Elsie is depicted in a full-length composition, clothed in a quaint dress within a seemingly natural setting, in keeping with the revival of interest in 'grand manner' eighteenth-century portraiture as a vehicle for bestowing status on the sitter and their family. For the nouveau riche, particularly in Britain but no less in newly federated Australia, portraits with references to the art of the past could suggest a cultured, wealthy lineage.[42]

Light, life and landscape

Elsie, daughter of H.W. Brooks, Esquire was exhibited at the Royal Academy in 1904 and, although characteristic of Fox's society portraiture at the time, contrasts sharply with the light-filled impressions of urban life and landscape that

he also exhibited. He had first become interested in French
Impressionism while in Europe in the 1880s, inspired by
the atmosphere, colour and mark making of artists such
as Whistler, Monet, Turner and the British Impressionist
Philip Wilson Steer. Fox travelled to Europe for the
second time in 1901, after receiving the National Gallery
of Victoria's commission, under the Gillbee bequest, for
an Australian history painting – required, ironically,
to be painted in London. He left Melbourne somewhat
disgruntled by the reception of his European-influenced
impressions of the Australian landscape.[43]

Following Fox's marriage to British-born painter Ethel
Carrick in Britain in 1905, the pair travelled widely
through Europe, painting high-key impressions of
European life on small portable boards *en plein air*.
They depicted bourgeois leisure and urban life in popular
holiday destinations such as the French coastal town of
Trouville, as in Fox's *Promenade* c. 1909. Working side
by side, they influenced each other's approaches to
rendering light and colour and for a time their work was
very similar, with small distinguishing features, such as
the additional details in Carrick's depictions of the era's
fashions. In 1908 they visited Australia together, where
they painted beaches and cosmopolitan scenes such as
Carrick's *The quay, Milsons Point* 1908. On hearing of an
art-market boom in Australia, they sought an Australian
audience for their European work.[44]

Long-term expatriate Rupert Bunny also returned briefly
to Australia in 1911, his first visit since his departure in
1884, with a selection of his recent French paintings.
Bunny had first travelled to Europe to study figure painting
under French Academic figure painter Jean Paul Laurens,
and did not return to Australia permanently until 1933.

Bunny was one of the most successful Australian
expatriates in France in his own time, aided by a firm

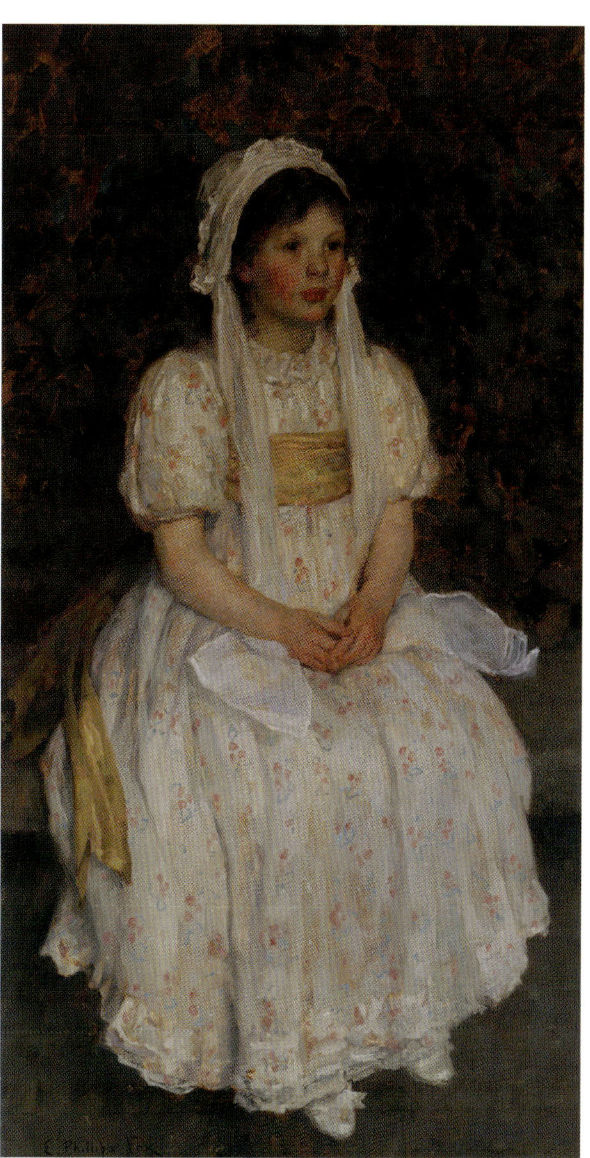

E. Phillips Fox
Elsie, daughter of H.W. Brooks, Esquire 1904
oil on canvas, 136.5 x 71.3 cm
National Gallery of Australia, Canberra, purchased 1963

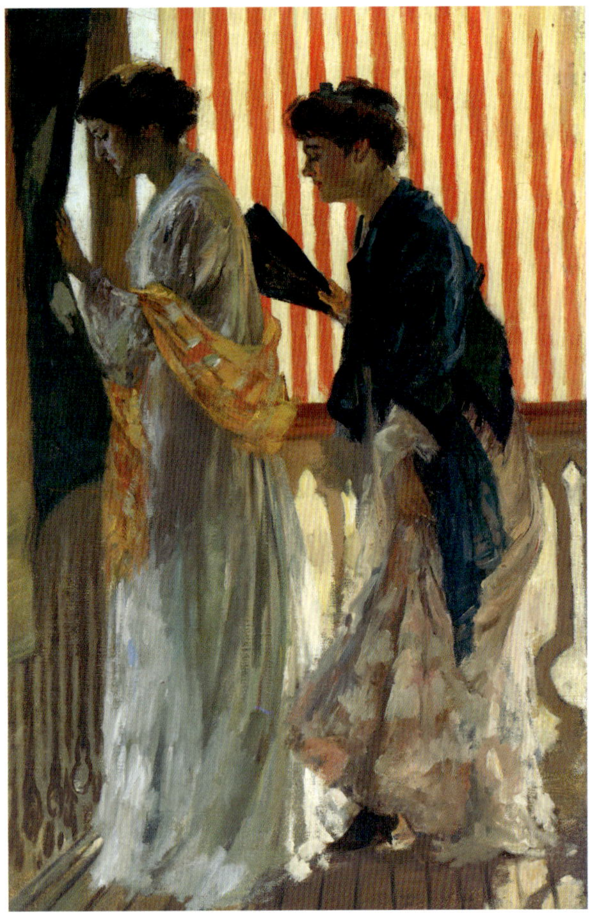

Rupert Bunny
Qui vient? [*Who comes?*] c.1908
oil on canvas, 81 x 54.2 cm
National Gallery of Australia, Canberra, bequest of John B. Pye 1963

command of the French language and early successes in the Old Salon in Paris. He has become most well known for the sumptuous compositions of women at leisure in gardens and interiors that he painted during this era.[45] Images of women and children had become increasingly popular in the major exhibitions, and many of the larger works from this series were also exhibited at the New Salon.[46] These paintings reveal Bunny's intuitive feeling for colour and his pleasure in the effects of light.

Despite the dominance of portraiture, figure painting and impressions of urban life, Arthur Streeton continued to paint landscapes while in Britain. He sought to come to terms with the constantly changing atmosphere, light and colour by drawing on the work of the nineteenth-century British Romantic landscape painters, particularly Turner and Constable. Shortly after his arrival in London in 1897, he wrote jubilantly to Tom Roberts that on seeing the works of Constable, Turner and Old Masters such as Titian: 'I feel convinced that my work hereafter will contain a larger idea & quality than before'.[47] Streeton journeyed through Britain in the footsteps of Constable, painting in locations such as Hampstead Heath. *View of Hampstead Heath from Jack Straw's Castle* c.1901–08 depicts the damp British atmosphere and poetic Turneresque effects of sunlight through fog.

His earlier enthusiasm notwithstanding, Streeton found it immensely difficult to establish himself in London. At the end of 1906, he returned to Australia for several months, keen to gauge the enthusiasm for his British work and to re-establish a relationship with the Australian market. In a Sydney newspaper interview, he expressed his delight in returning to Australia. He likened it to 'a recall to a golden-haired mistress after years of banishment', and extolled the virtues of the colours of the Australian landscape, for which Britain, he felt, was no match.[48]

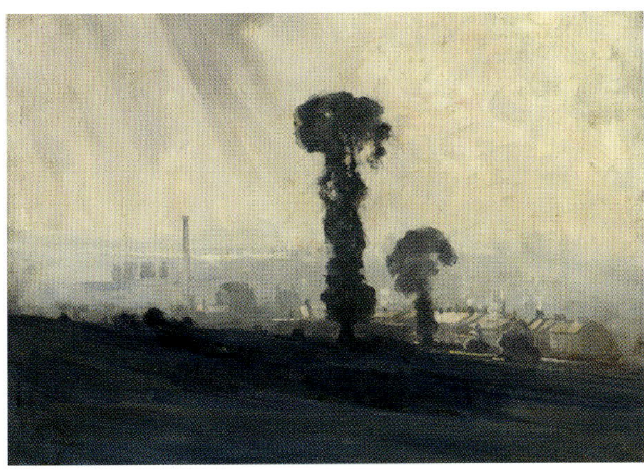

Arthur Streeton
View of Hampstead Heath from Jack Straw's Castle c. 1901–08
oil on canvas, 35.5 x 45.9 cm
National Gallery of Australia, Canberra, bequest of Mary Meyer in memory of her husband Dr Felix Meyer 1975

The success of Streeton's exhibitions in Melbourne and Sydney in 1907, particularly with his Australian subjects, likely prompted the visits of a number of other expatriates in subsequent years. Streeton returned to London in 1907 and, as well as exhibiting successfully in Britain, he worked to maintain a relationship with the Australian market, sending works back and returning home again for a short visit in 1914.

Home and away

Expatriate painters during the Federation years were living in Europe as citizens of Australia for the first time. Their relationship with their homeland varied greatly, with many still considering themselves British. A number of major artists were already overseas by the time of Federation, and thus experienced the particularities of this era's excitement and quest for national identity at a

remove. Indeed, most expatriates were concerned with producing art that appealed to their European audience rather than presenting Australian trends in an international context.

Expatriate connections with Australia were maintained through return visits to teach, paint and share their experiences, as well as by sending works back for sale and exhibition. Their achievements were widely reported in the newspapers, often with extensive listings of works accepted into the major European exhibitions. When Tom Roberts wrote home about the success of having a portrait (*Madame Hartl* 1909–10) hung 'on the line', at eye height, for the first time rather than 'skied', his entire letter was reproduced in a Melbourne paper.[49]

Correspondence between artists and family members across the globe also provides insight into personal stories of inspiration, success and hardship. While some artists lived overseas for long periods during this time, and indeed some never returned, others experienced periods of acute homesickness. 'I found a little dried gum leaf in my things the other day,' Ramsay wrote home from his small studio in Paris, 'Lambert & I nearly went mad over the thing as we burnt it & imagined we were back there in the bush, boiling the Billy.'[50]

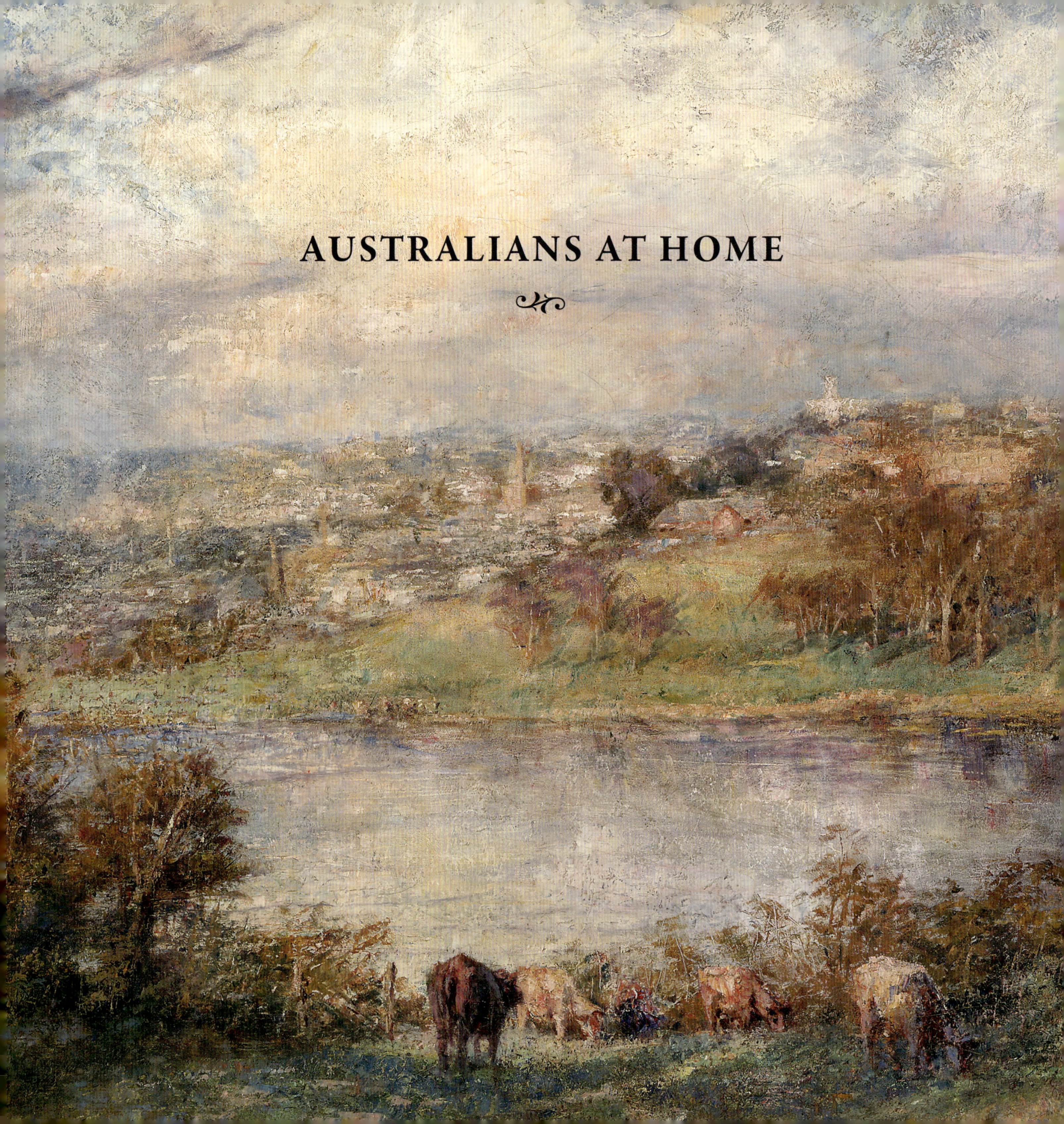

AUSTRALIANS AT HOME

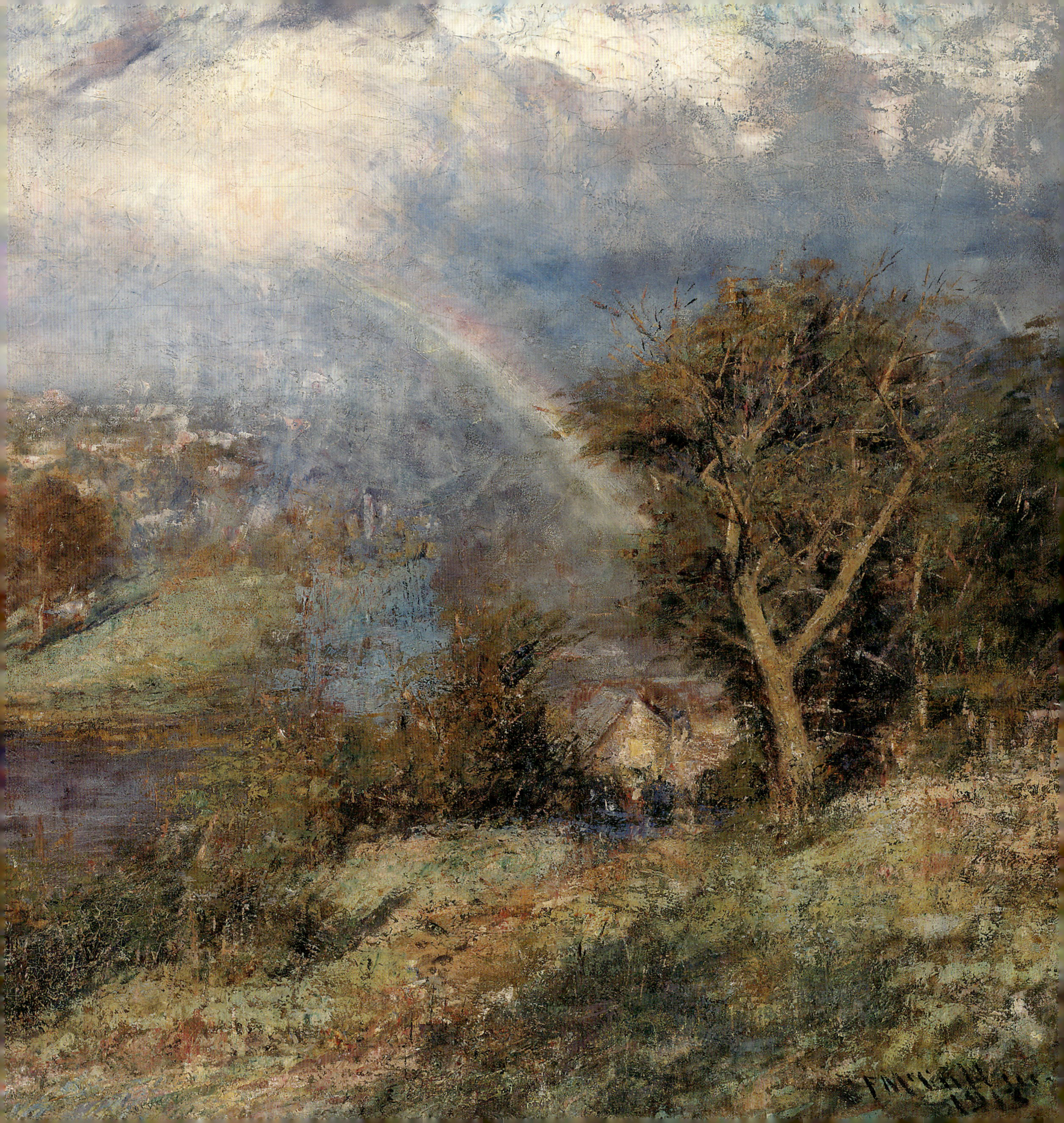

born Australia 1865 died Australia 1915
Europe, England 1887–92, 1901–13
Harvesting c. 1900
painted in Melbourne
oil on canvas, 49 x 120.7 cm
National Gallery of Australia, Canberra, purchased 2005

What struck us on entering the studio was the light that seemed to emanate from the pictures … the dull room, with dingy hangings, appeared full of windows, out of which one gazed into the most exquisite bits of scenery … the dull room seemed lighted by the pictures.
(*Arena*, 20 October 1900)

'In art everything must start from the springboard of nature', Fox noted on his return to Melbourne in 1913 (*Argus*, 21 May 1913). 'One may treat nature realistically, decoratively, or as a basis for the expression of ideas, but nature must be there. The Impressionists, Manet, Monet, Degas, Sisley, Pissarro, and the rest of them had a very fine, true feeling for nature … Monet, painting his haystacks in different effects – what a fine protest it was against the art which manufactures little pictures in the studio without reference to nature! … Not that I condemn painting in the studio. One must go to nature to learn, as before nature one is objective, a servant. But in the studio one paints to express oneself, and must be a master.'

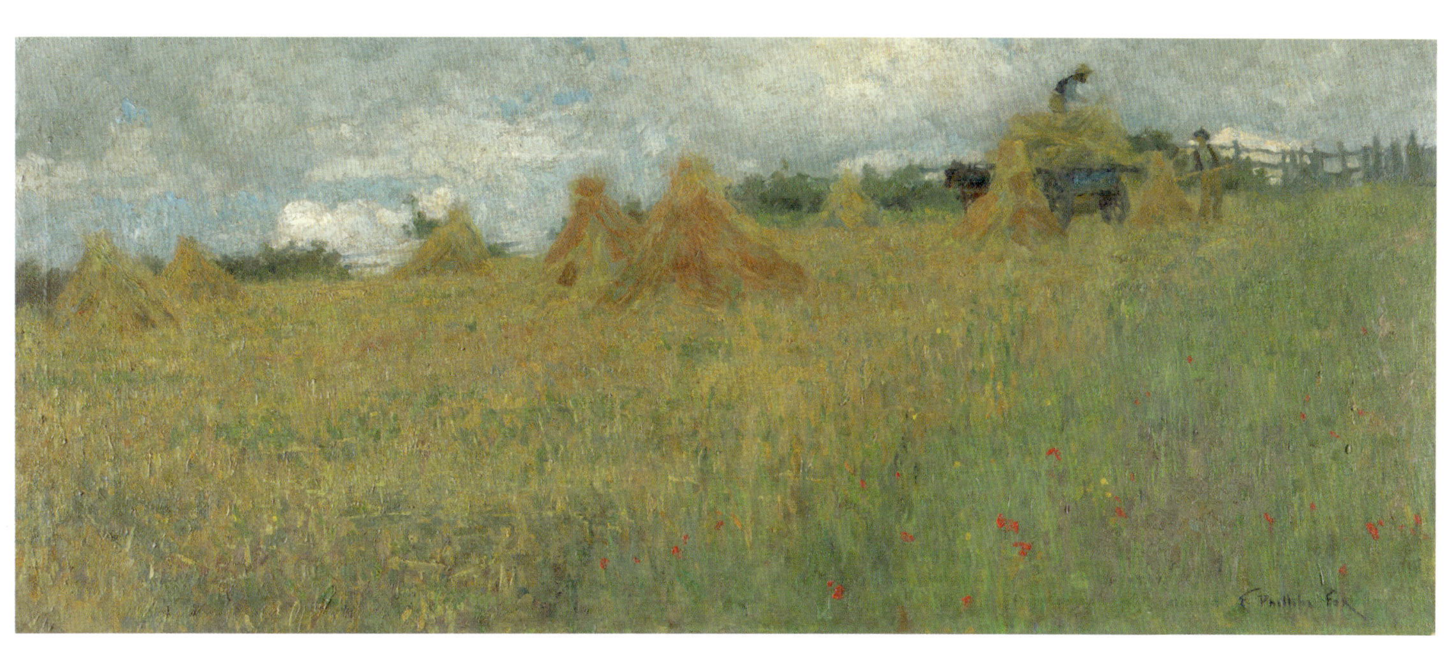

born Australia 1861 died Australia 1940
The old shed c. 1900
painted in Warrandyte, Victoria
oil on canvas, 36.6 x 28.2 cm
National Gallery of Australia, Canberra, purchased 2003

To be a bush woman and artist in one is no rare combination in the colonies. Hence we have Miss Clara Southern, whose works have adorned the walls of many well-known Commonwealth galleries. Her bush experiences give her work an added charm …
(*Brisbane Courier*, 25 November 1905)

Clara Southern was associated with the Australian Impressionists, studying under Frederick McCubbin at the National Gallery School in Melbourne in the 1890s, and accompanying her contemporaries on painting day-trips to Heidelberg. Southern settled in the semi-rural Victorian region of Warrandyte, in the Yarra Valley, in 1905, encouraging a range of artists to visit and live in the region over the subsequent decades.

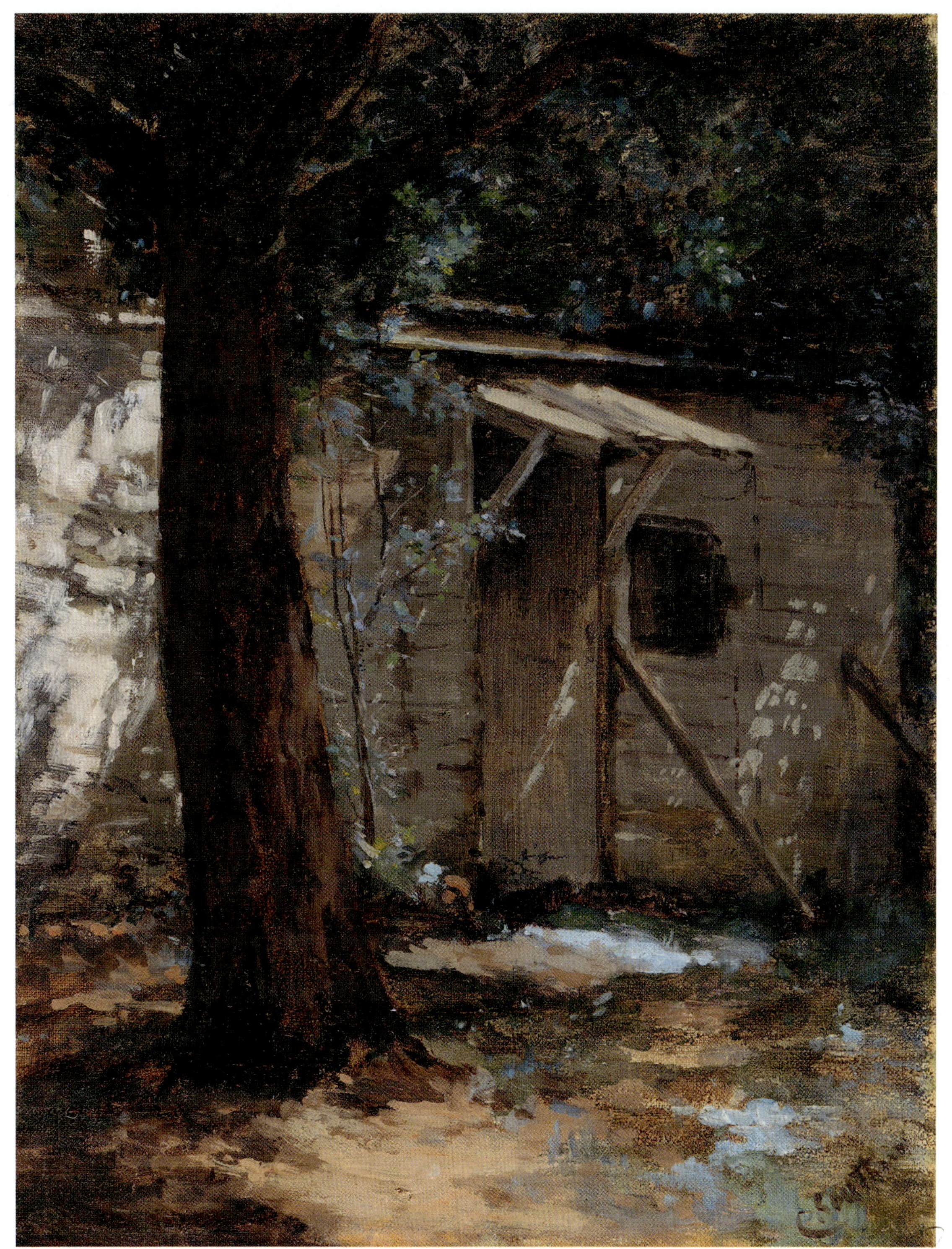

born Australia 1855 died Australia 1917
Triumphal Arch at Princes Bridge, Melbourne 1901
painted in Melbourne
oil on pine panel, 26 x 34.4 cm
National Gallery of Australia, Canberra, given by Hugh McCubbin to the Commonwealth
as a first-hand record of a great historical event and to mark the centenary of the birth of
Frederick McCubbin 1955

*The arches rose over the great masses of the people in the gorgeousness of their colours
like so many rainbows set against a cloudless sky. The senses were whirled away with the
bewildering spectacle, and for moments together buildings, people and arches alike were
blended in a dizzy hundred-tinted wave of colour.*
(*Age*, 7 May 1901)

Painted on-the-spot, *Triumphal Arch at Princes Bridge, Melbourne* conveys the
infectious public jubilation surrrounding Federation. In 1908, following his return
from Europe, Frederick McCubbin revisited this subject in the *Arrival of Duke and
Duchess of York, Melbourne, 1901* 1908 (National Gallery of Victoria, Melbourne),
with a striking, confident approach in the manner of J.M.W. Turner, further
dramatising the arch.

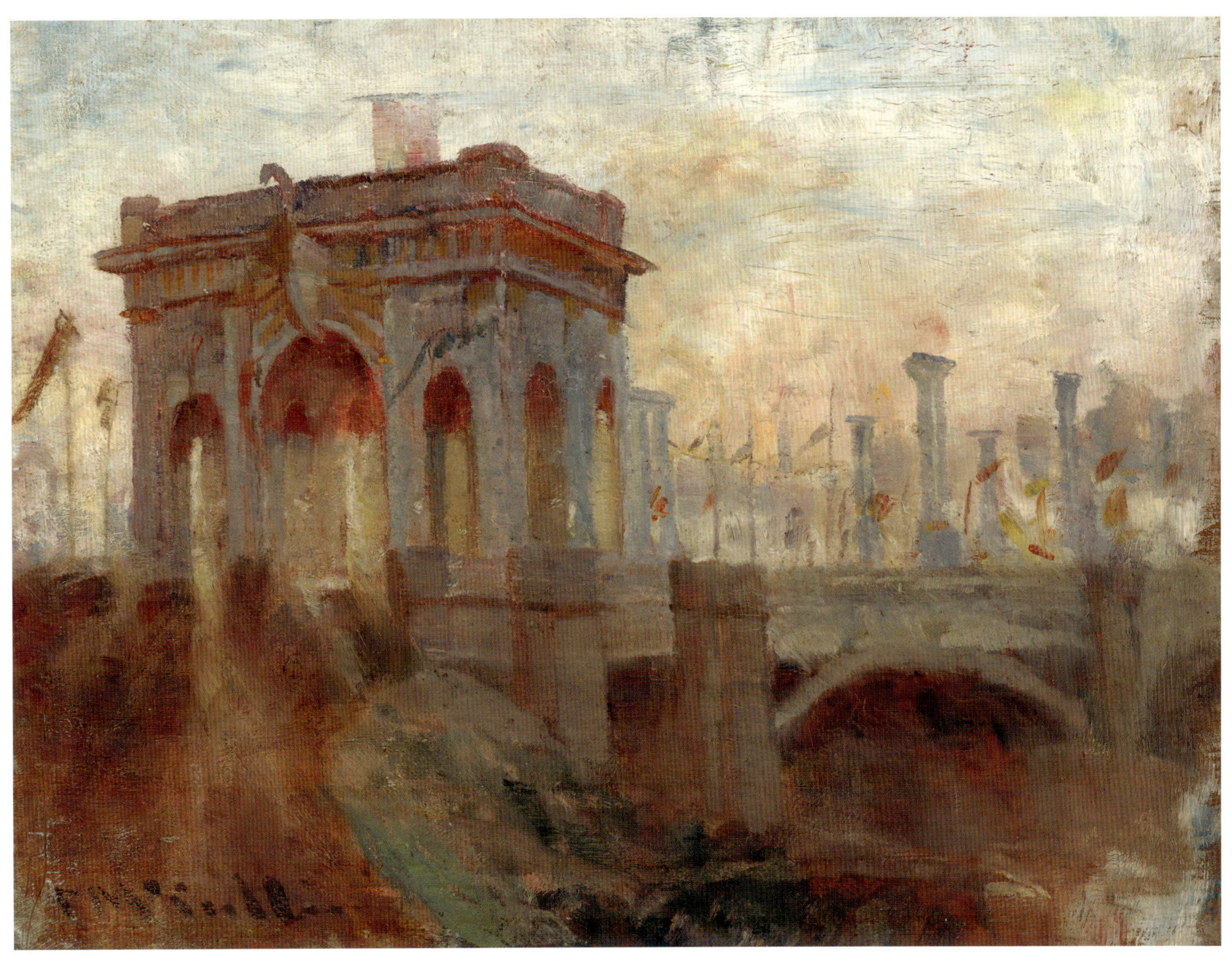

born England 1856 died Australia 1931
Australia from 1869; England, Europe 1881–85, 1903–23
Sketch for 'Opening of Federal Parliament', 1901 1901
painted in Melbourne
oil on academy board, 30.3 x 45.6 cm
National Library of Australia, Canberra

The atmosphere was radiant and illuminated the vast spaces of the building and the great sea of faces with a bright Australian glow. A sight never to be forgotten was the assemblage which, in perfect order but with exalted feeling, awaited the arrival of the Duke and Duchess in the great avenues which branch out from beneath the vast dome of the Exhibition Building.
(*Argus*, 10 May 1901)

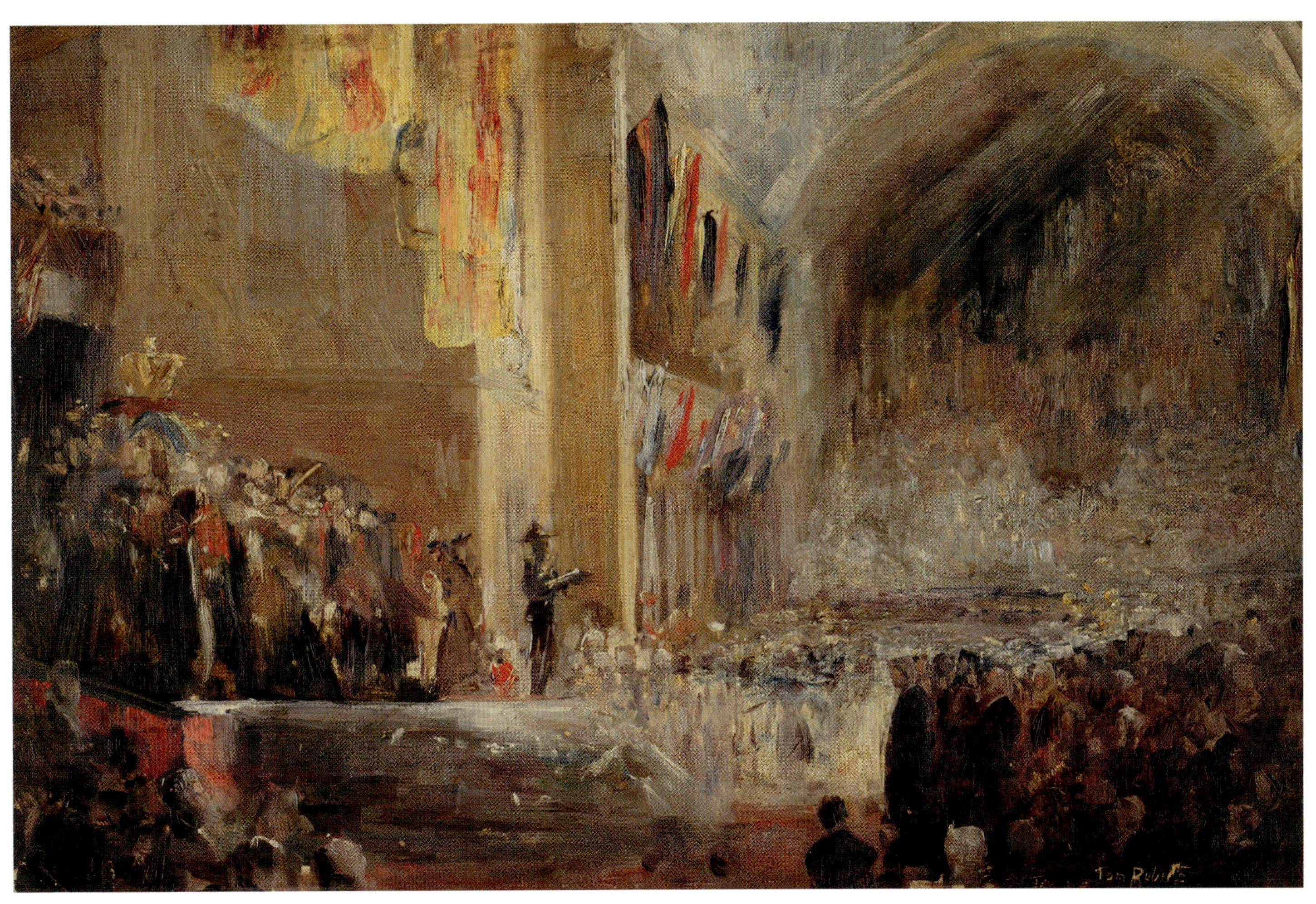

born England 1856 died Australia 1931
Australia from 1869; England, Europe 1881–85, 1903–23
Sketch portrait – Senator J.T. Walker 1901
painted in Melbourne
oil on canvas mounted on cardboard, 9.2 x 7.9 cm
National Gallery of Australia, Canberra, purchased 1976

A deputation, consisting … yesterday waited upon Mr J .T .Walker, and presented him with a requisition, signed by 6500 electors of New South Wales, asking that he would offer himself as one of the six candidates to be elected to a seat in the Federal Senate … Mr Walker, in reply, thanked the deputation for the confidence placed in him, as evidenced by the numerously signed requisition … He said that, whether elected or not, he should always consider that he had been paid the greatest possible compliment …
(*Sydney Morning Herald*, 23 January 1901)

Scottish-born banker, Senator J.T. Walker was elected as one of the first six Australian senators to represent New South Wales in the first Federal Parliament. He was returned to office over four elections until his retirement from politics in 1913. This lively sketch was just one of the many individual portraits Roberts completed in preparation for 'the big picture'. Roberts travelled widely within Australia before departing for London to request sittings with several of the city's dignitaries, principally the Duke of Cornwall and York.

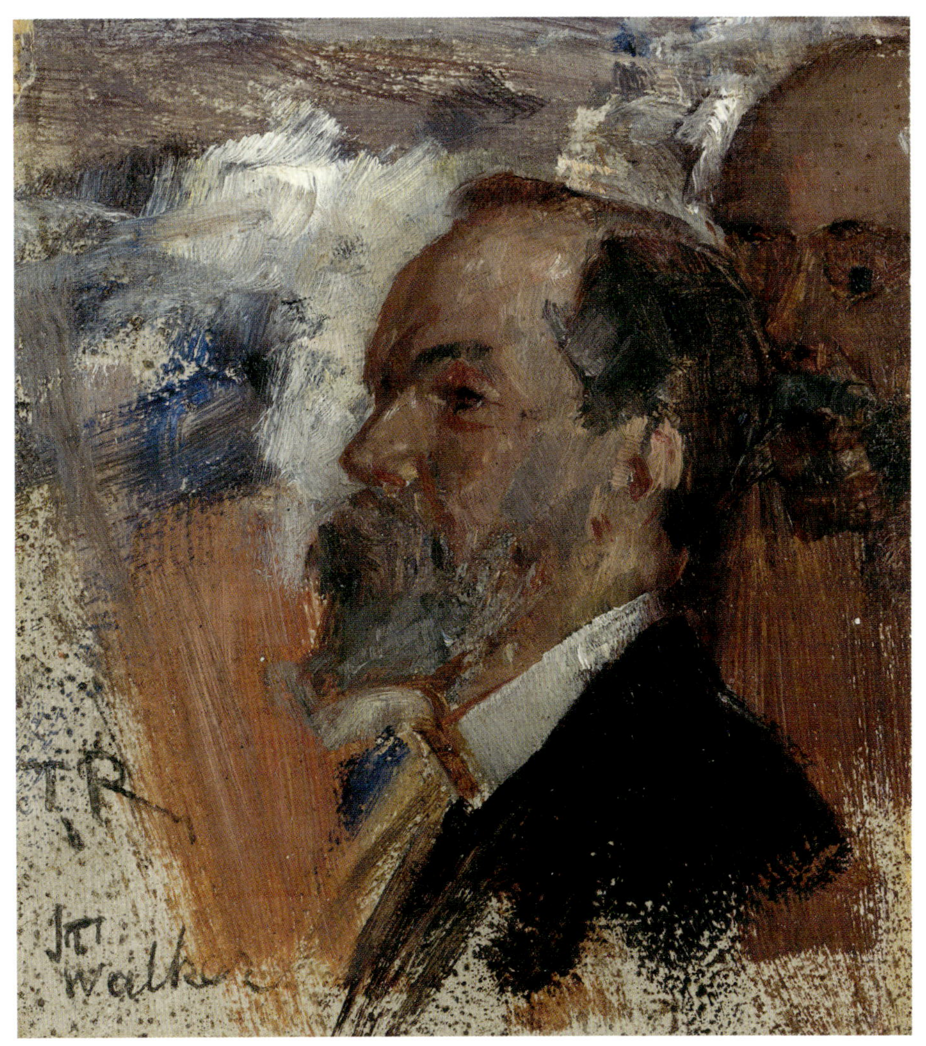

born Germany 1877 died Australia 1968
Australia from 1884; Europe, England 1899–1903
The saplings 1904
painted in Adelaide
oil on canvas, 120.5 x 90.3 cm
National Gallery of Australia, Canberra, bequest of Millie Hay Joyner 1993

'The design of the gum' noted Hans Heysen, 'is expressed in the flow of its trunk and limbs, and the design of the European tree mainly in its foliage. In Europe the great masses of foliage first attract the eye, here the limbs and trunk, which, on account of their proportion and colour, make themselves felt first, and one thinks of the foliage as a secondary matter.'

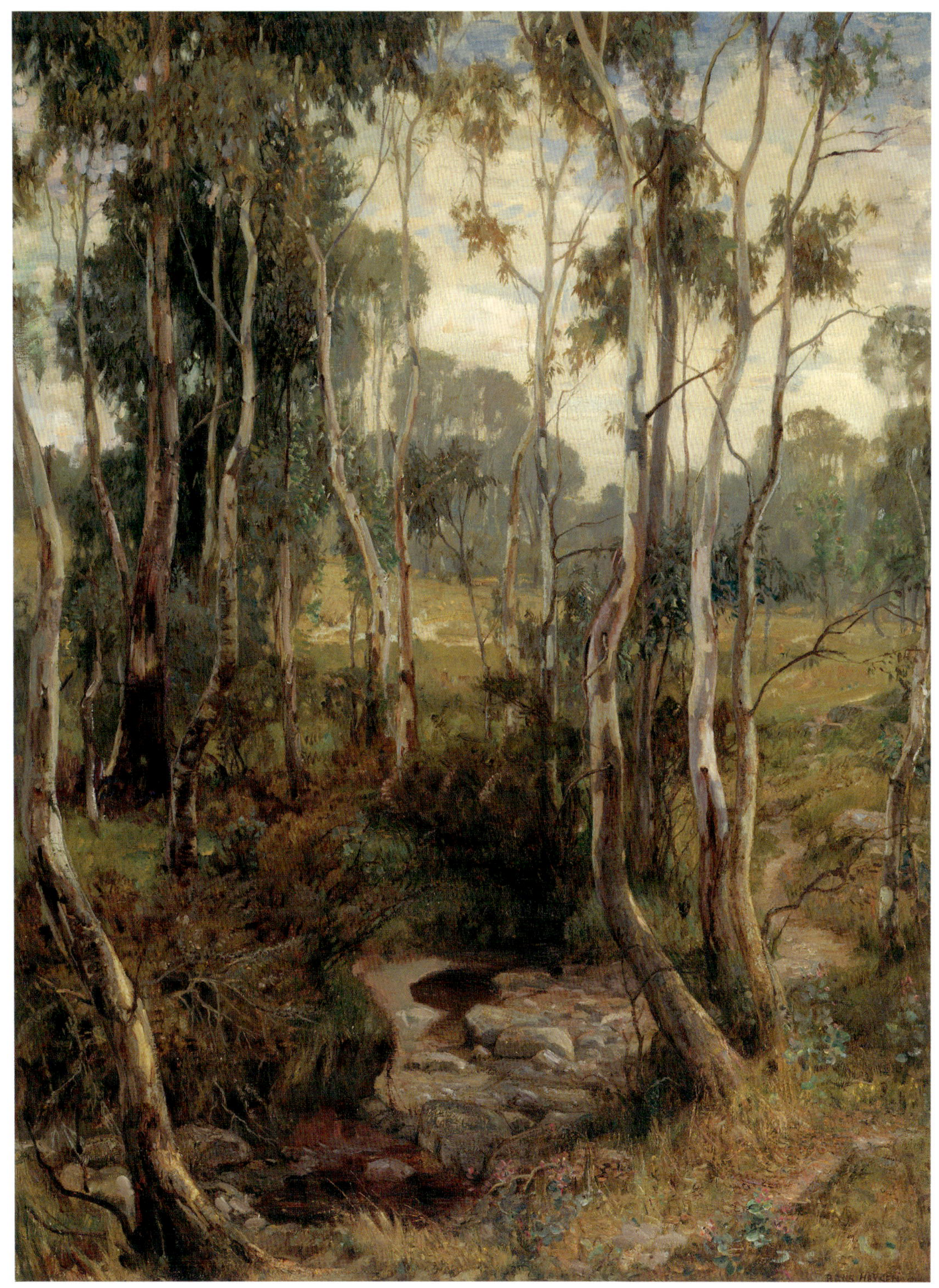

FLORENCE FULLER

born South Africa 1867 died Australia 1946
Australia from c. 1875; South Africa 1892–94; France, England 1894–1904; India 1909–11
Dawn landscape c. 1905
painted in Perth
oil on canvas, 44.5 x 60 cm
National Gallery of Australia, Canberra, purchased 2011

And the last night-shadow ebbs
From the trees like a falling tide,
And the dew-hung spiderwebs
On the grass-blades spread far and wide –

Each sharp spike loaded well,
Bent down low with the heavy dew –
Wait the daily miracle
When the world is all made anew:

When the sun's rim lifts beyond
The horizon turned crystal-white,
And a sea of diamond
Is plain to the dazzled sight.

At the dawning of the day,
To my happiness thus it fell:
That went the common way,
And witnessed a miracle.
(*Dawn* by Dorothea Mackellar[2])

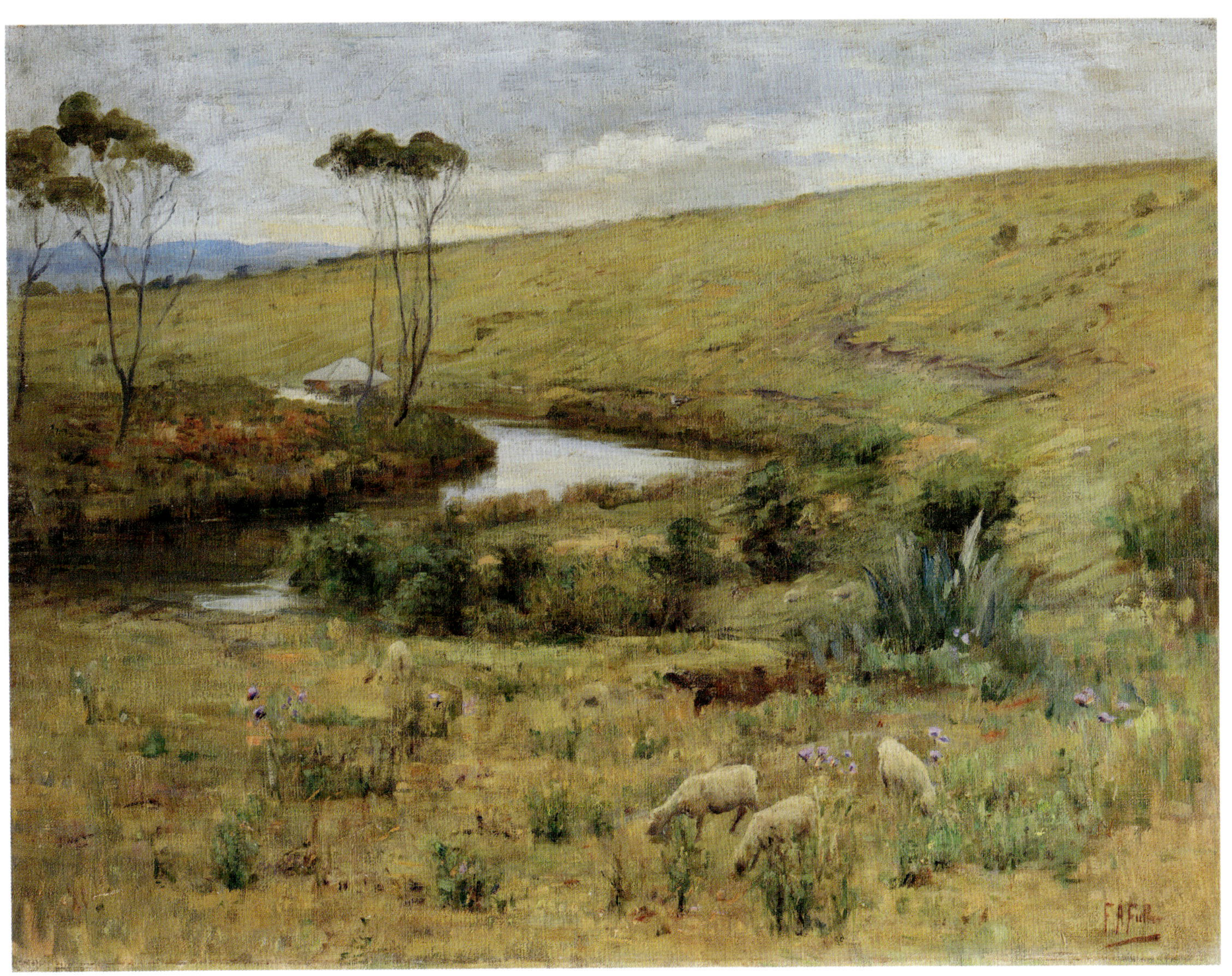

born England 1959 died England 1925
Australia 1889–1925
Wisteria, Coochin Coochin 1905
painted at Coochin Coochin homestead, Queensland
oil on wood panel, 25.7 x 16.9 cm
National Gallery of Australia, Canberra, purchased 2008

Godfrey Rivers arrived in Australia from England in 1890, settling in Brisbane.
He became an influential teacher, and was a key figure in establishing the Queensland
Art Gallery. His article, 'Sunlight in pictures', published in the *Queensland Art Society
Annual Report* (1898), reflects his interest in the idea of an 'Australian school' of
painting and the significance of the landscape in his own art:

> There is no doubt that close and intelligent observation of nature in its varying
> moods would soon lead us to strike out into new paths and to express ourselves
> more in harmony with our natural surroundings …[3]

In *Wisteria, Coochin Coochin*, Rivers delights in the colour of both native and
introduced flora, a key feature of this Queensland homestead garden. *Coochin
Coochin* is the oldest surviving homestead in Queensland. The elaborate garden was
established by Gertrude Bell (widow of James Bell), and opened to visitors after 1905.
Bell held annual garden parties, charity events and hosted many visitors, including
Agatha Christie, Laurence Olivier and the Prince of Wales.[3]

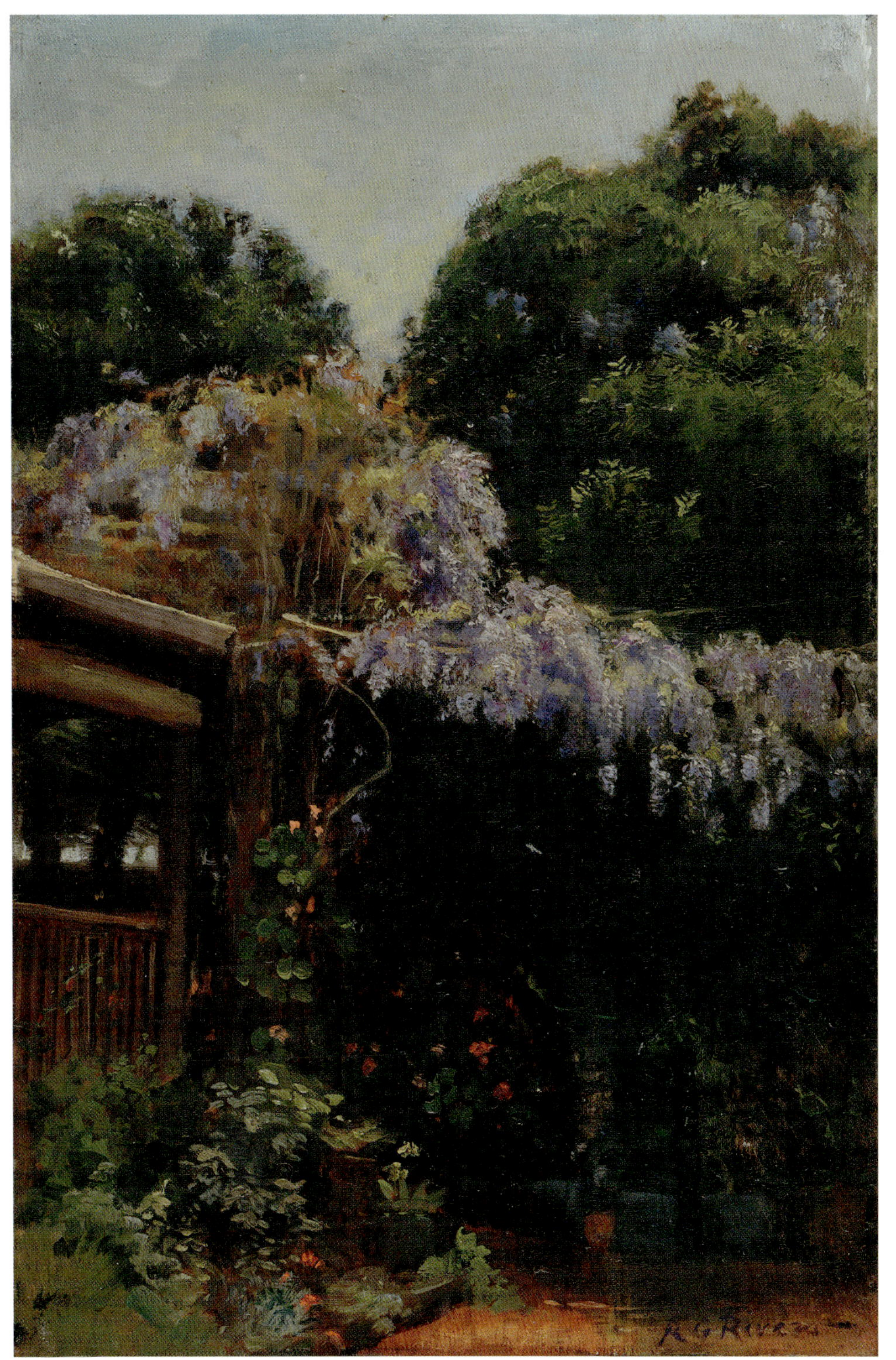

born Australia 1878 died Australia 1910
The drover 1906
most likely painted near Orange, New South Wales
oil on canvas board, 60.8 x 45.4 cm
National Gallery of Australia, Canberra, purchased 1972

I love a sunburnt country,
A land of sweeping plains,
Of ragged mountain ranges,
Of droughts and flooding rains.
I love her far horizons,
I love her jewel-sea,
Her beauty and her terror –
The wide brown land for me!

Core of my heart, my country!
Her pitiless blue sky,
When sick at heart, around us,
We see the cattle die –
But then the grey clouds gather,
And we can bless again
The drumming of an army,
The steady, soaking rain.
(Verses from *My country* by Dorothea Mackellar[5])

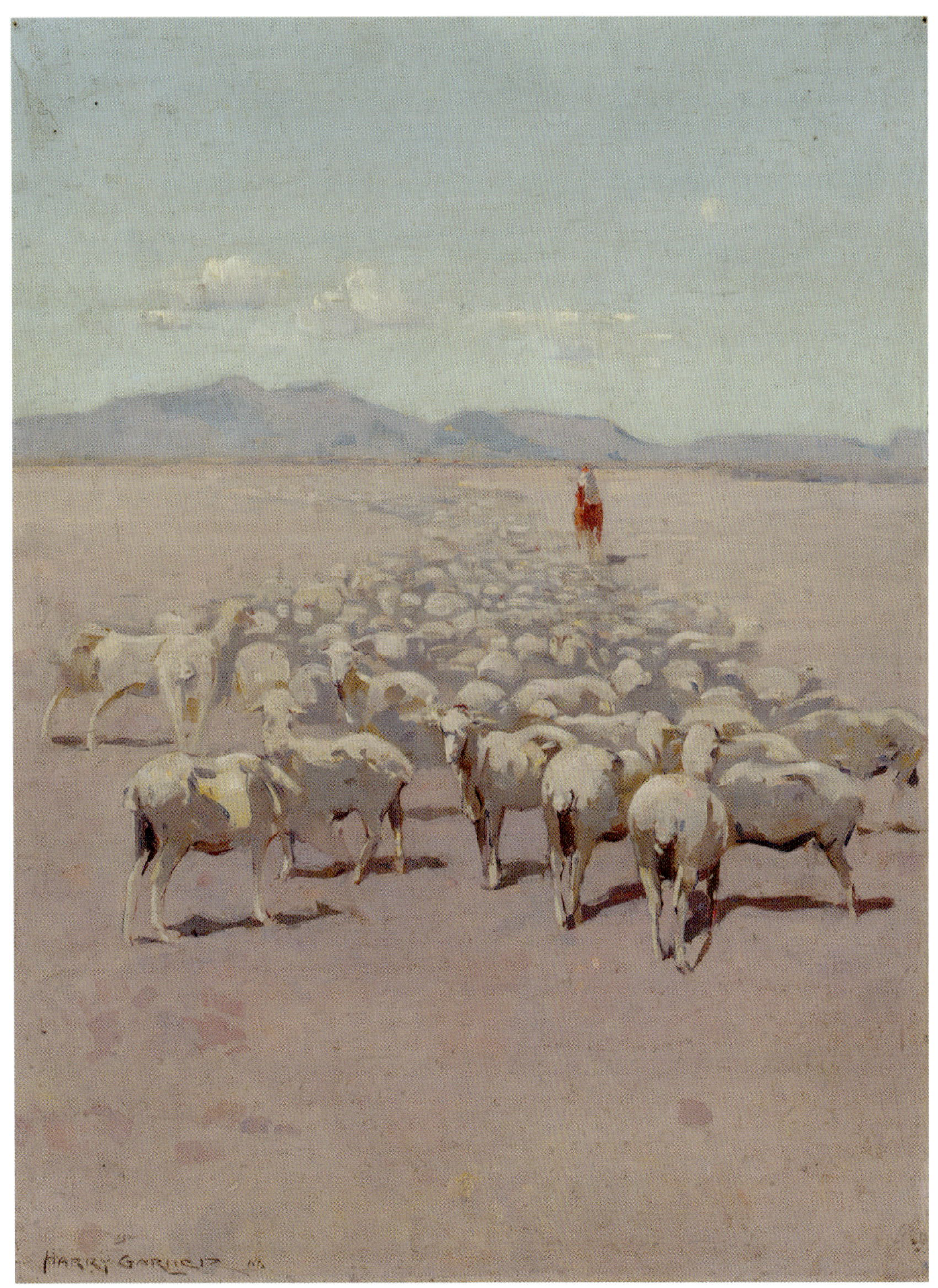
HARRY GARLICK

born Australia 1871 died England 1955
England 1910–21, 1922–25 and from 1952
Flamingoes c. 1907
painted in Sydney
oil on canvas, 30.6 x 61 cm
National Gallery of Australia, Canberra, acquired with the assistance of the
Masterpieces for the Nation Fund 2006

Corot said: 'I dream my picture, and later on paint my dream'. *Sydney Long, responsive
to the varying moods of nature also dreams under such influence and portrays for us in
a convincing manner his harmonies of colour and pattern with added decorative qualities.
Sensitive and selective to a degree he unerringly weaves the composition with precision in
a satisfying design, never commonplace.*
(B.J. Waterhouse, *Sydney Long A.R.E., loan exhibition*, 1941)

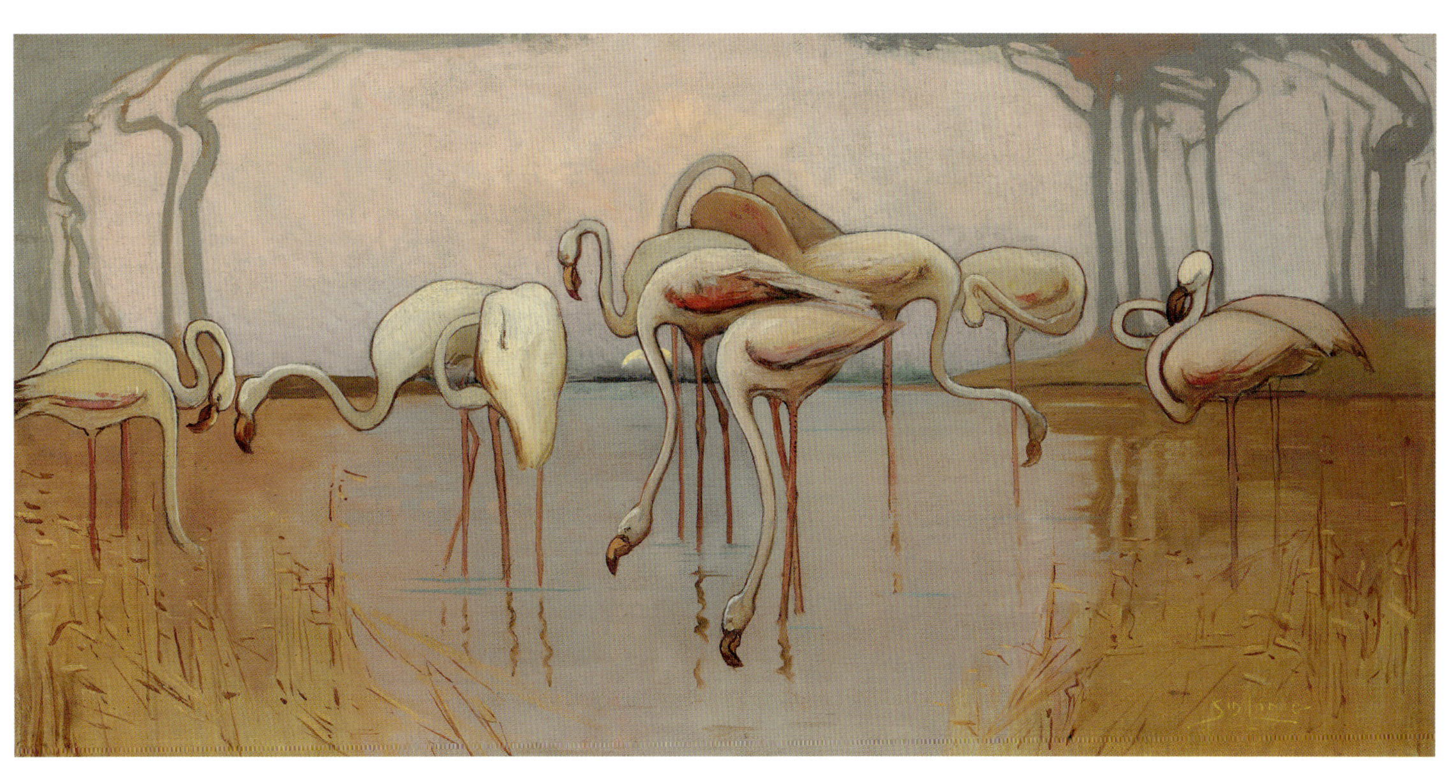

FREDERICK MCCUBBIN

born Australia 1855 died Australia 1917
The broken fence 1900–07
painted in Melbourne
oil on canvas, 138 x 168 cm
National Gallery of Australia, Canberra, purchased 1959

In the nineteenth century it was a common practice to dress children in red so as to spot them easily in the bush. Images of children in the bush had became a preoccupation in Australian art and literature, prompted by a long-held and often too real fear that they would get lost.

It is likely that the model for this boy was Frederick McCubbin's son, Sydney, who would have been about four years old when the painting was started in 1900.[6] *The broken fence* was painted over a period of seven years, as McCubbin was an artist 'who could not leave a painting alone – he constantly returned to it, to refine it, to "perfect" it.'[7] The predominantly grey-green palette and soft brush effects reflect his work of the early Federation years, with touches of the brighter greens characteristic of works painted after his time in Europe in 1907.

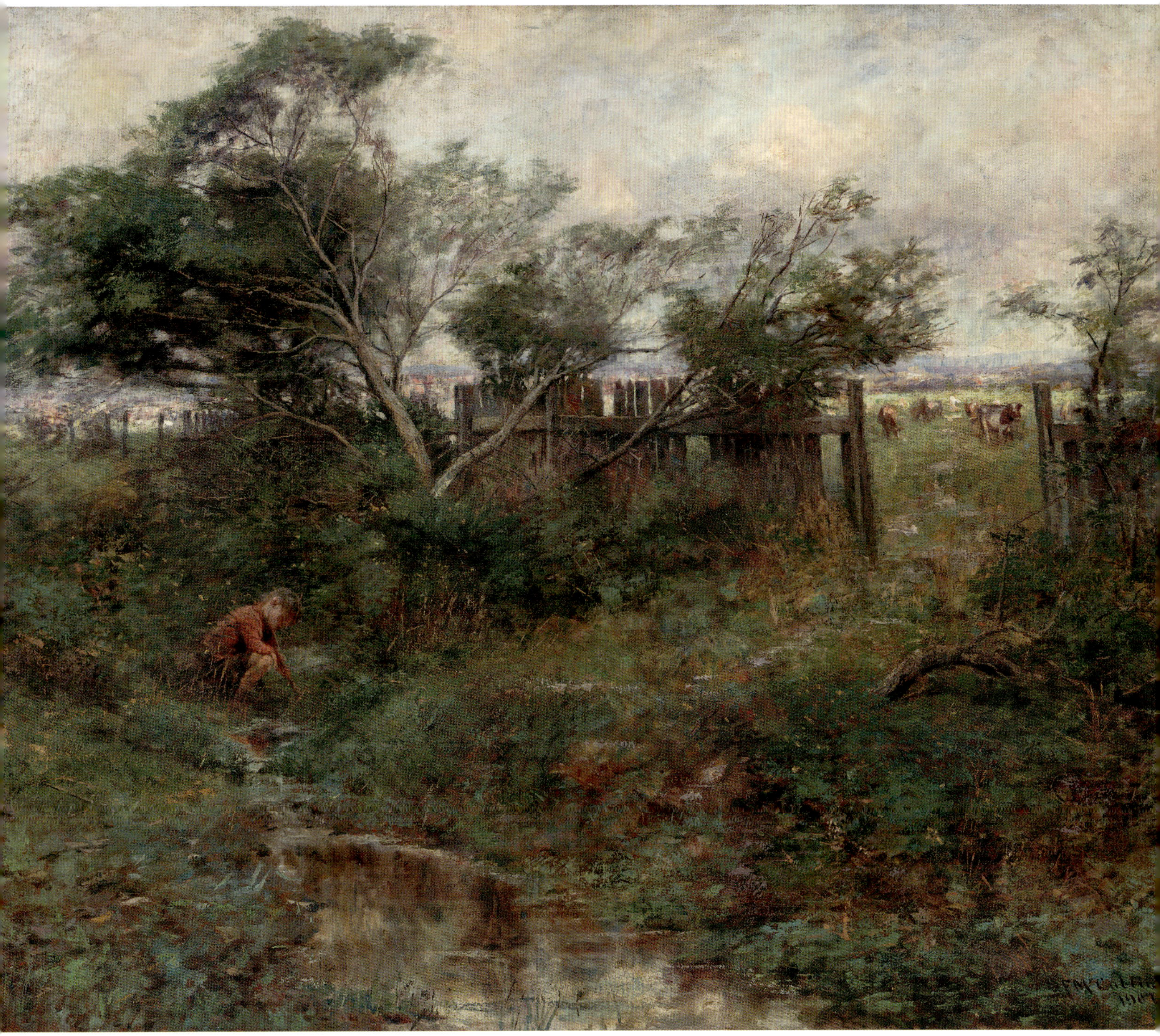

born Australia 1836 died Australia 1914
England 1898, 1900
Near Liverpool, New South Wales c. 1908
painted in Sydney
oil on canvas, 74.2 x 125 cm
National Gallery of Australia, Canberra, acquired with the assistance of the
Masterpieces for the Nation Fund 2005

A Romantic realist, W.C. Piguenit was inspired by a love of the Tasmanian and
New South Wales landscapes. The most senior painter working at the turn of
the century, Piguenit's work spans the late colonial years through to the end of
the Federation era.

A report on Piguenit's address at the Art Gallery of New South Wales 1891 Annual
banquet appeared in the *Sydney Morning Herald* (7 September 1891). Summarising
Piguenit, the article noted that: 'A few years ago we were told that our birds were
without song, our flowers without perfume, and the Australian landscape was a
landscape of unbroken and unrelieved monotony'; thereafter reflecting on the artist's
delight that Australian perceptions were changing, with increasing recognition of the
'beauties in our valleys and forests and mountains and plants which were well worthy
of the highest efforts of the artist's brush and of the poet's song … building
up a school which would be national in its character.'

Near Liverpool, New South Wales was painted in the early years of the twentieth
century. It reflects Piguenit's increasing shift away from the sublime to capturing
atmospheric weather effects and the play of light.

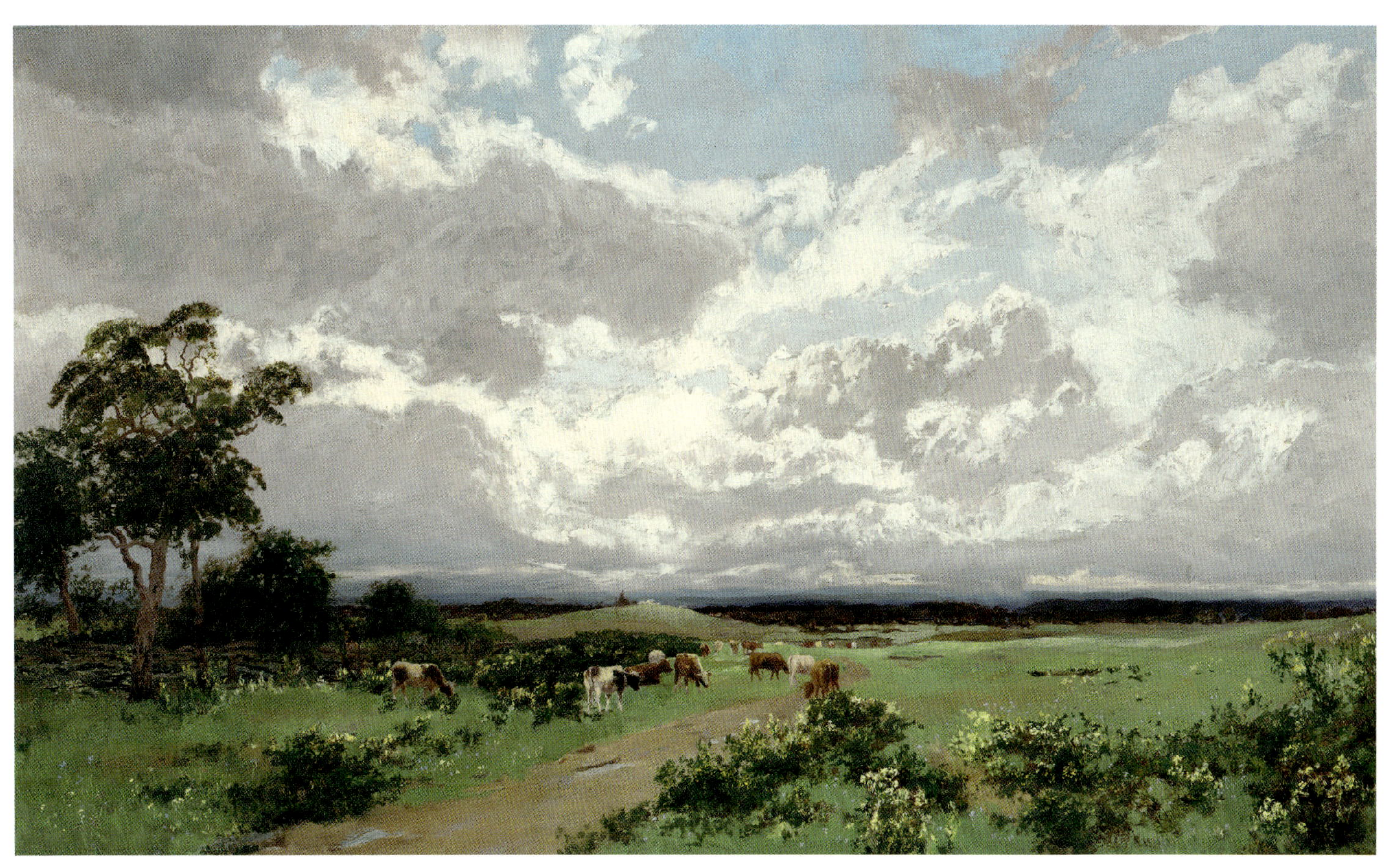

born England 1872 died Australia 1952
France from 1905; Australia 1908, 1913–16, with frequent visits thereafter
The quay, Milsons Point 1908
painted in Sydney
oil on artists' board, 26.4 x 34.9 cm
National Gallery of Australia, Canberra, purchased 1975

English-born and trained, Ethel Carrick visited Sydney for the first time in 1908 with her Australian husband and fellow artist, E. Phillips Fox. Carrick painted numerous impressions of Australian beaches, urban life and leisure in the manner of her light-filled European travel images, revelling in Australia's bright sunlight and the era's fashions.

[A] word or two to those who perhaps haven't rightly understood the value of impressionistic art. Sometimes one hears 'but it isn't finished'. If the critic would stop and reflect, she would consider that if the subject represents moving figures, so-called finish means arrested movement. When you go out on the street and see a familiar moving crowd, try and remember how much (or how little) detail you see when the people are moving.
(Ethel Carrick, quoted in the *Register*, 14 July 1925)

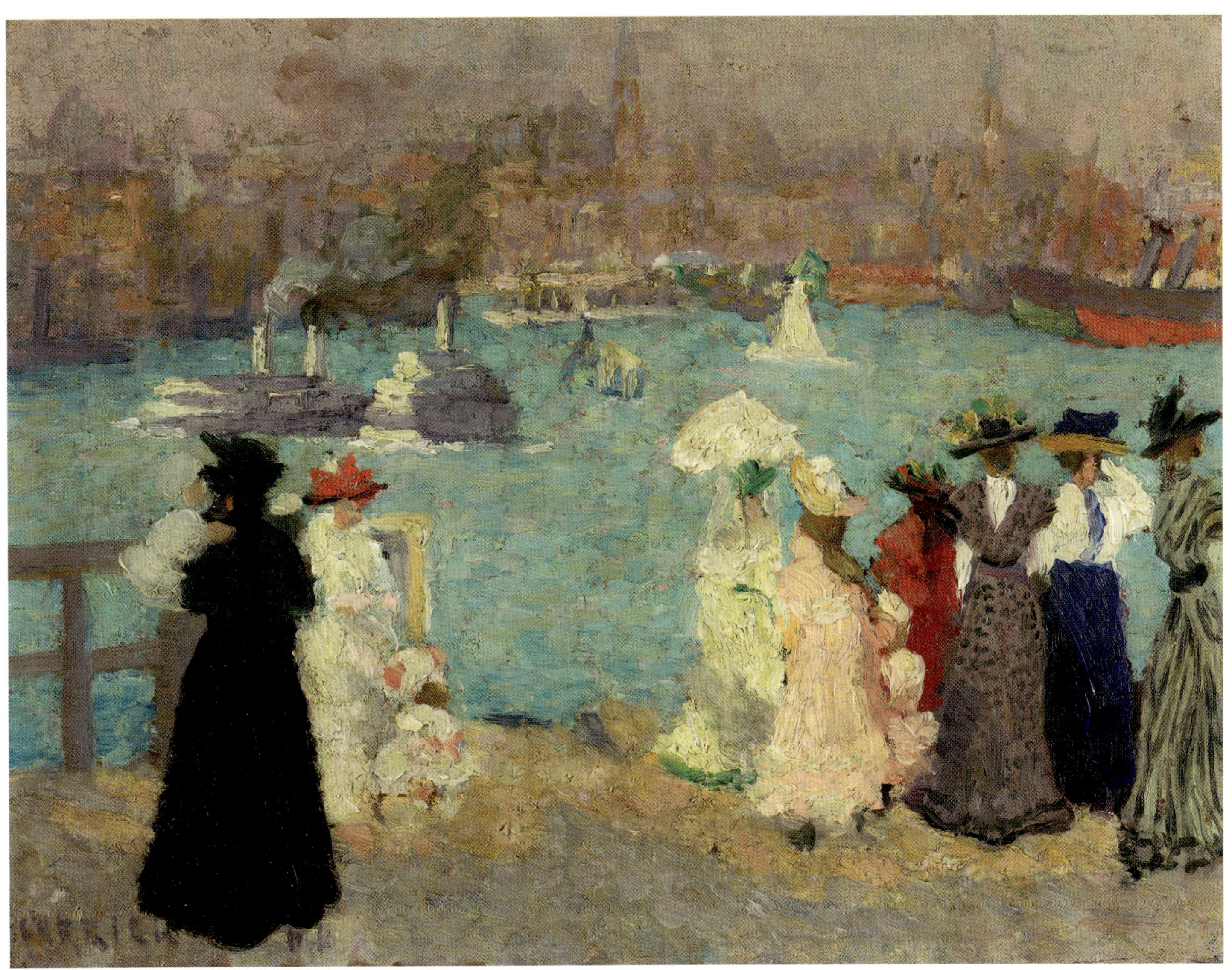

FREDERICK MCCUBBIN

born Australia 1855 died Australia 1917
Ships, Williamstown c. 1909
painted in Williamstown, Victoria
oil on canvas-textured paper board, 25.6 x 35.8 cm
National Gallery of Australia, Canberra, gift of Philip Bacon AM 2010

McCubbin commented enthusiastically to Tom Roberts in a letter (27 January 1909):

> I have been down at Williamstown for a few pochards [painted sketches]
> my dear boy, just like Venice, lovely colour – water and sky and an old slip …[7]

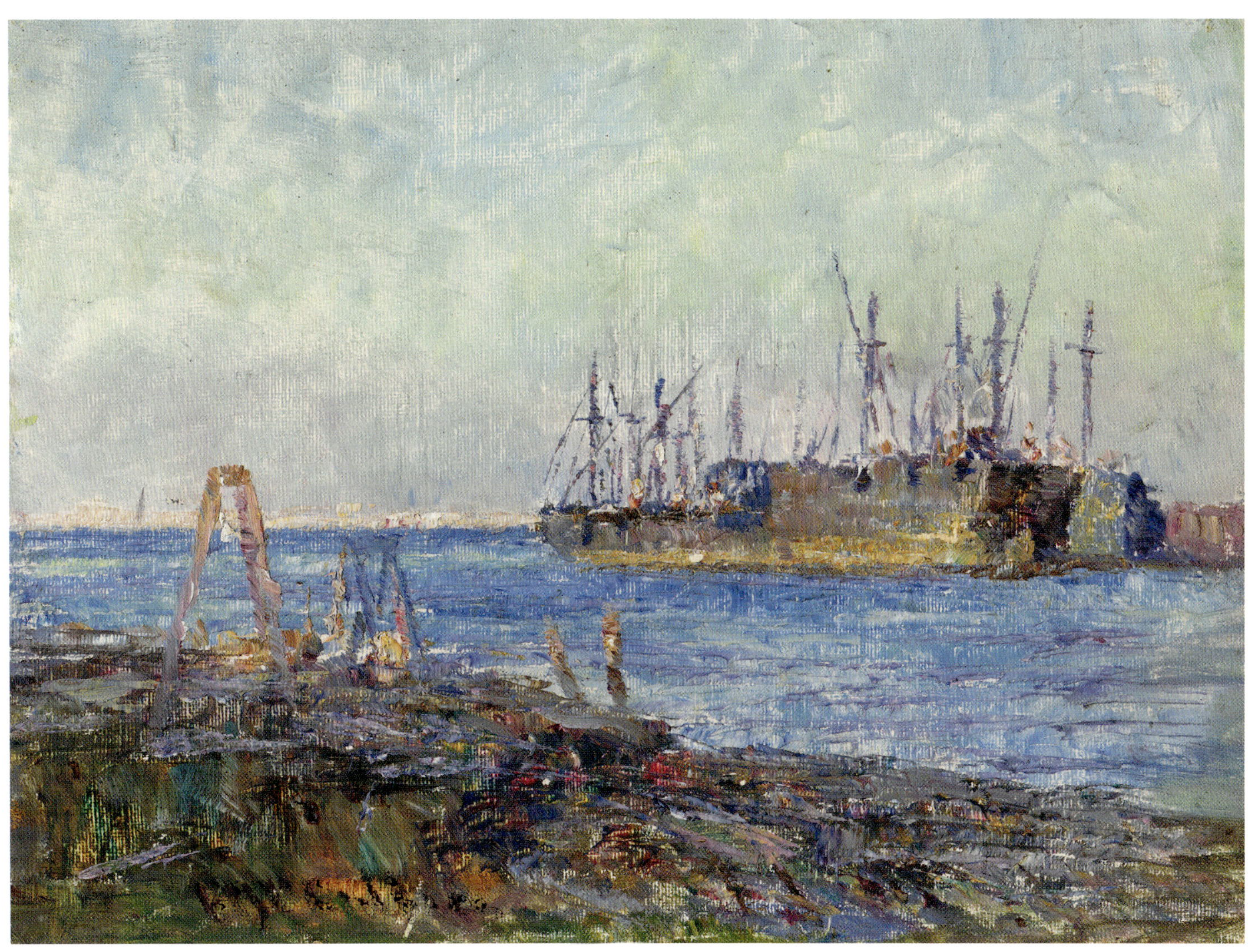

born England 1869 died Australia 1947
Australia from 1896; England 1907–08
A winter's day on the Swan c. 1910
painted in Perth
oil on canvas, 61.5 x 91.8 cm
National Gallery of Australia, Canberra, purchased with funds from the Ruth Robertson
Bequest 2011, in memory of Edwin Clive and Leila Jeanne Robertson

Locally Mr. Linton's work is almost so well known as to render comment superfluous. As an artist his chief aim, and consequently his leading characteristic, is purity. He has a keen eye for atmospheric effects, for breezy firmaments, and clouds distinct with motion. He is fully alive to the value of a blue sky … Although by no means a slave to his colours, his inherent tastes impel him to greater activity at those hours and seasons when the sparse colouring of Australian landscapes takes on a deepened tone … 'A lover of art for art's sake,' happy in choice of subject and painstaking in his drawing and modelling.
(*West Australian*, 13 March 1907)

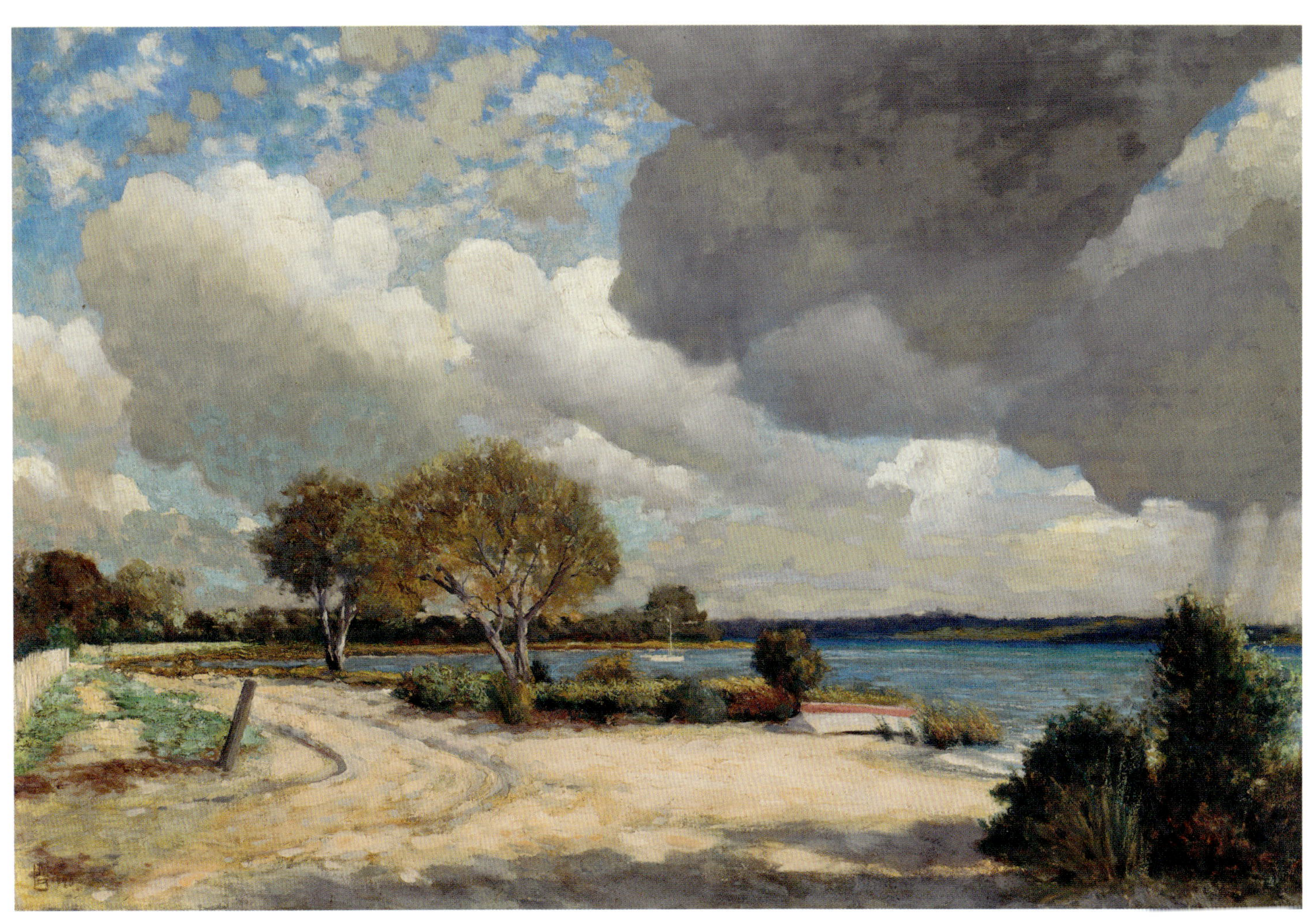

born Australia 1861 died Australia 1940
Audrey and Chicapick 1911
painted in Warrandyte, Victoria
oil on canvas, 43 x 56 cm
National Gallery of Australia, Canberra, gift of Jill Cahn and Judy Laver 2010

Miss Clara Southern (Mrs. J. Flinn) is a sweet and original singer of the Australian bush in colour, which, by the most skilful use of her pigments, she realises in all its beauty and charm, its majestic silences, its harmonies, and those mysterious distances we all know and feel when in its midst.
(*Argus*, 11 March 1914)

Audrey and Chicapick is a sensitive portrait of Professor Osbourne's young daughter Audrey (later Cahn) with the family's pet rooster. The Osbourne's property was close by where Clara Southern lived with her husband John Flinn in Warrandyte, Victoria. The quiet intimacy of this portrait would become a distinctive characteristic of Southern's work.

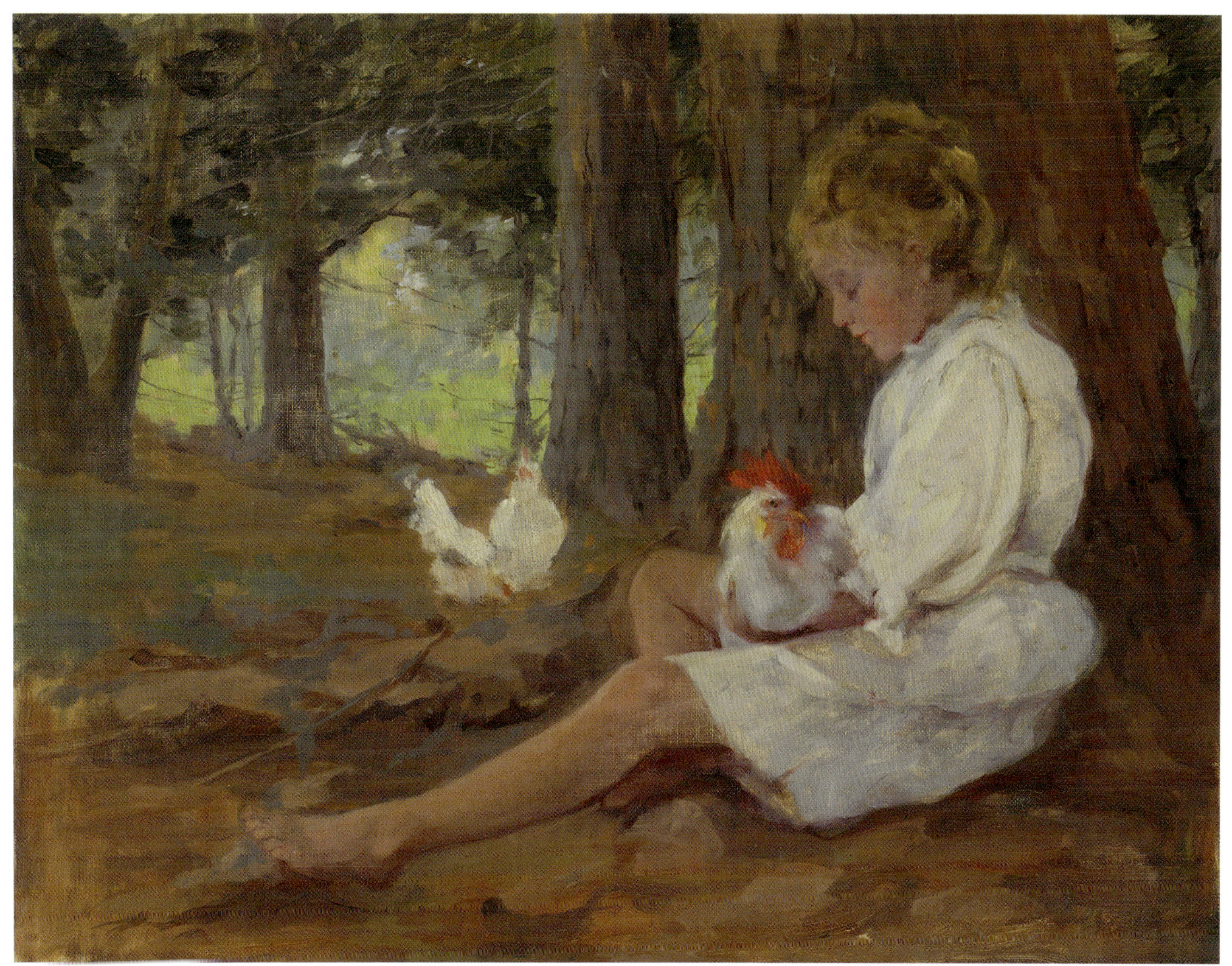

born Australia 1872 died Australia 1951
Europe 1889–95, 1935–37
The boy with the palette 1911
painted in Melbourne
oil on canvas, 175.5 x 108.5 cm
National Gallery of Australia, Canberra, gift of U.S. Teague 1976

In an article in *Table Talk* (25 July 1901) Violet Teague explained how she came to adopt art as a profession. Her engagement with great art began in childhood: 'When I was a child I had the chance of seeing the Spanish galleries, and never shall I forget Velasquez, with their beautiful horses and exquisite colouring, or the lovely Raphaels.' No doubt she enjoyed the company of Theo Scharf, the young subject of this portrait, who often worked beside Teague in her studio.

Despite the growing popularity of 'nation-building' images of the Australian landscape during the Federation era, Violet Teague is best known for her portraiture. *The boy with the palette* reveals the influence of her early training in Brussels and London, and became one of her most highly regarded works. *The boy with the palette* won praise from a *Sydney Morning Herald* reviewer (6 August 1913) when it was first shown at the Society of Women Painters Spring Exhibition.

Later in 1913, Teague successfully exhibited this work at the *Federal Art Exhibition* in Adelaide, and in 1920 submitted the portrait to the New Salon where it was awarded a silver medal. In 1921 the work was selected to hang 'on the line' at the Royal Academy in London, next to a full-length portrait by American-born, London-based painter John Singer Sargent.[8]

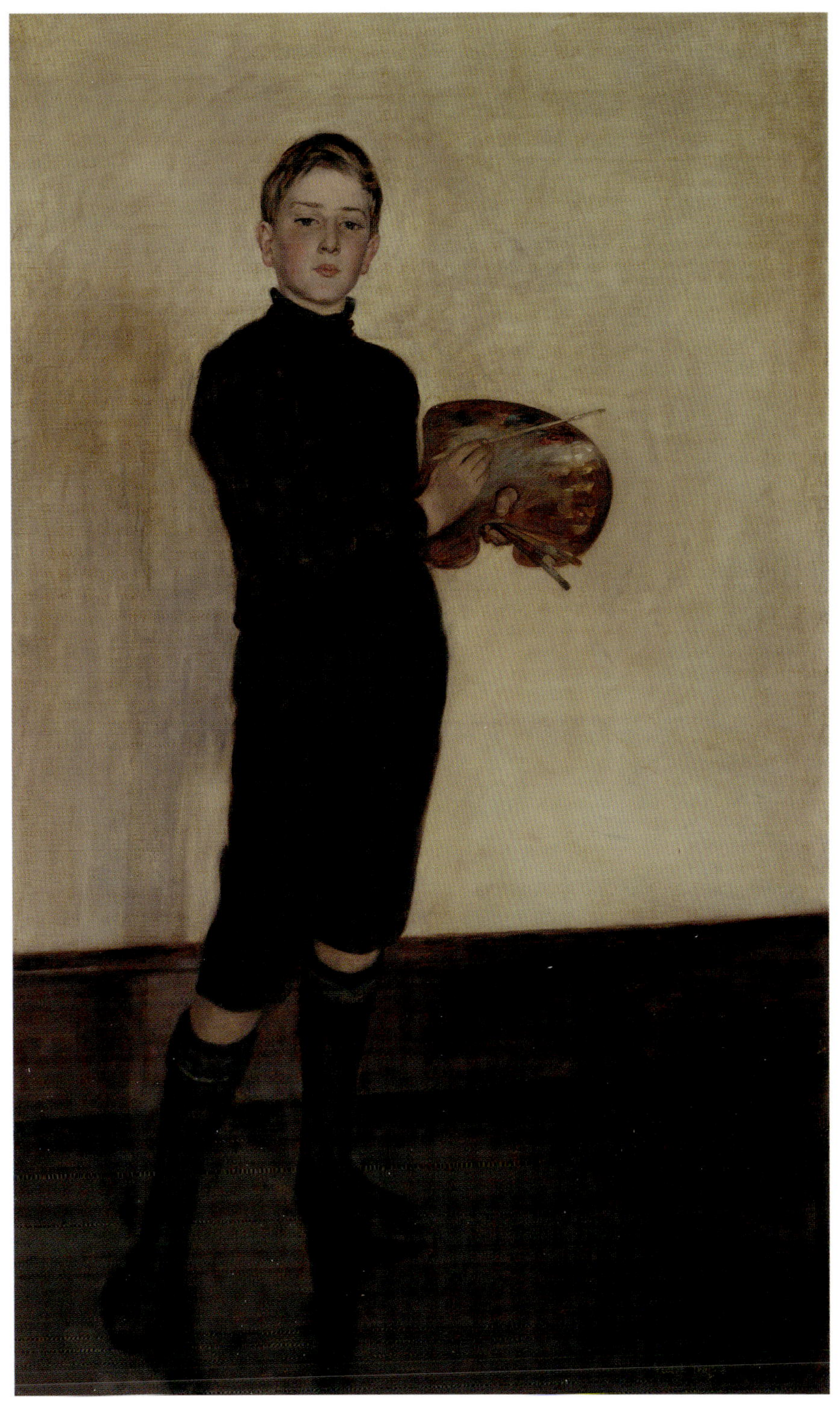

ELIOTH GRUNER

born New Zealand 1882 died Australia 1939
Australia from 1883; England 1924–25
Figures at Coogee 1913
painted in Sydney
oil on wood panel, 14.9 x 23.3 cm
National Gallery of Australia, Canberra, purchased 2009

In the catalogue for Elioth Gruner's 1983 retrospective, Gladys Lecky, the niece of a close friend of Gruner, is noted as recalling summer outings early in the artist's career. Lecky 'accompanied her uncle and Gruner ("Uncle Jean") on most weekends of the 1912–13 summer to the beach, with Gruner painting constantly until they were all sunburnt.'[10]

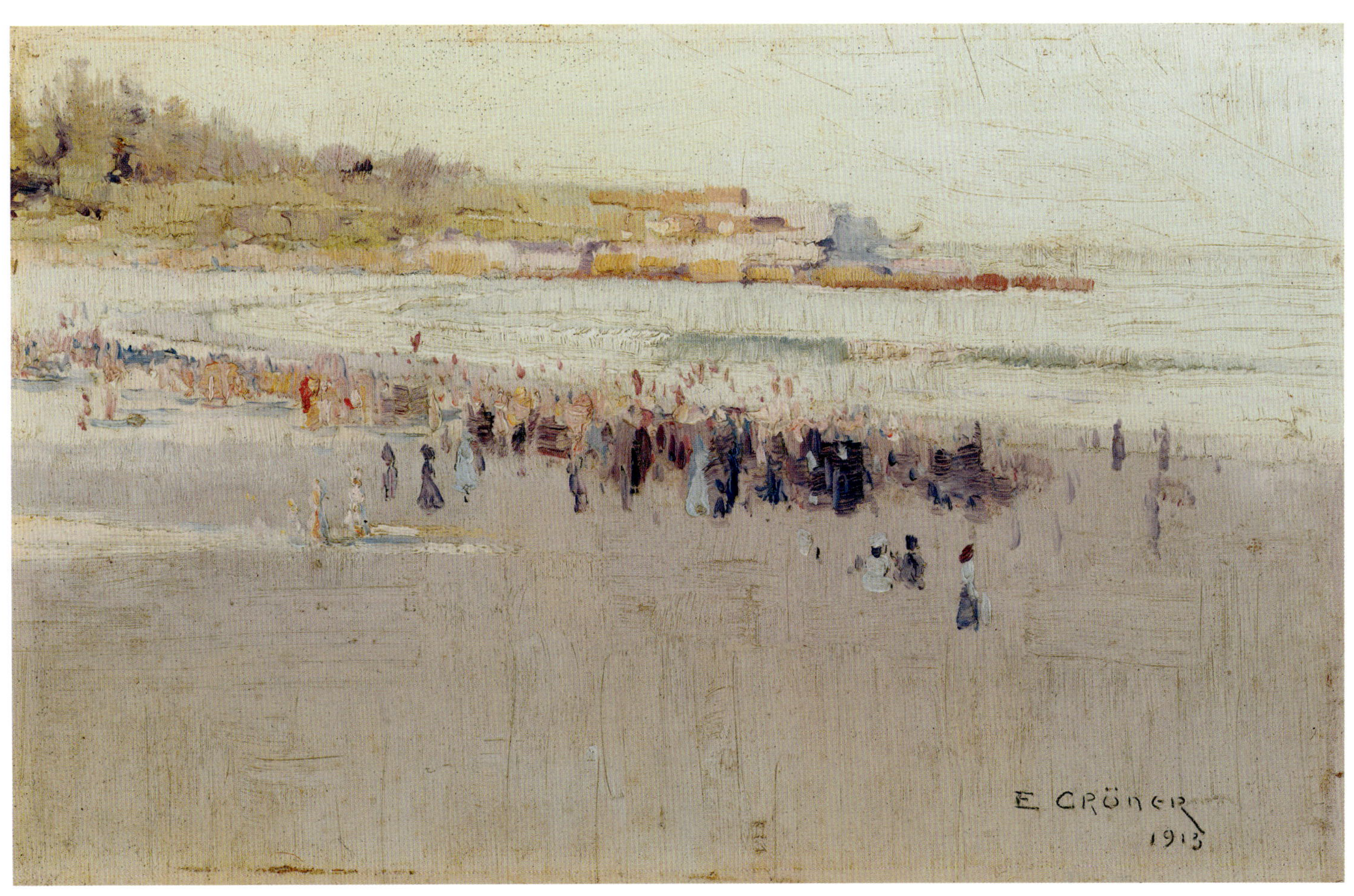

born Australia 1855 died Australia 1917
Flood waters 1913
painted in Melbourne
oil on canvas, 92.5 x 182 cm
National Gallery of Australia, Canberra, purchased 1973

'Nature under our Australian sky seems to me to be like a shy reserved person', McCubbin stated in an interview with the *Age* (10 February 1894), 'but you only have to wait and watch her varying moods, and you will find all the beauty you can desire.'

Flood waters depicts a view over the Yarra River from the property neighbouring McCubbin's home, on the outskirts of Melbourne. In 1916 he noted that it 'is precisely the pictures of things familiar to us, of homely subjects … which most appeal to us and more often therefore rise to true greatness.' [11]

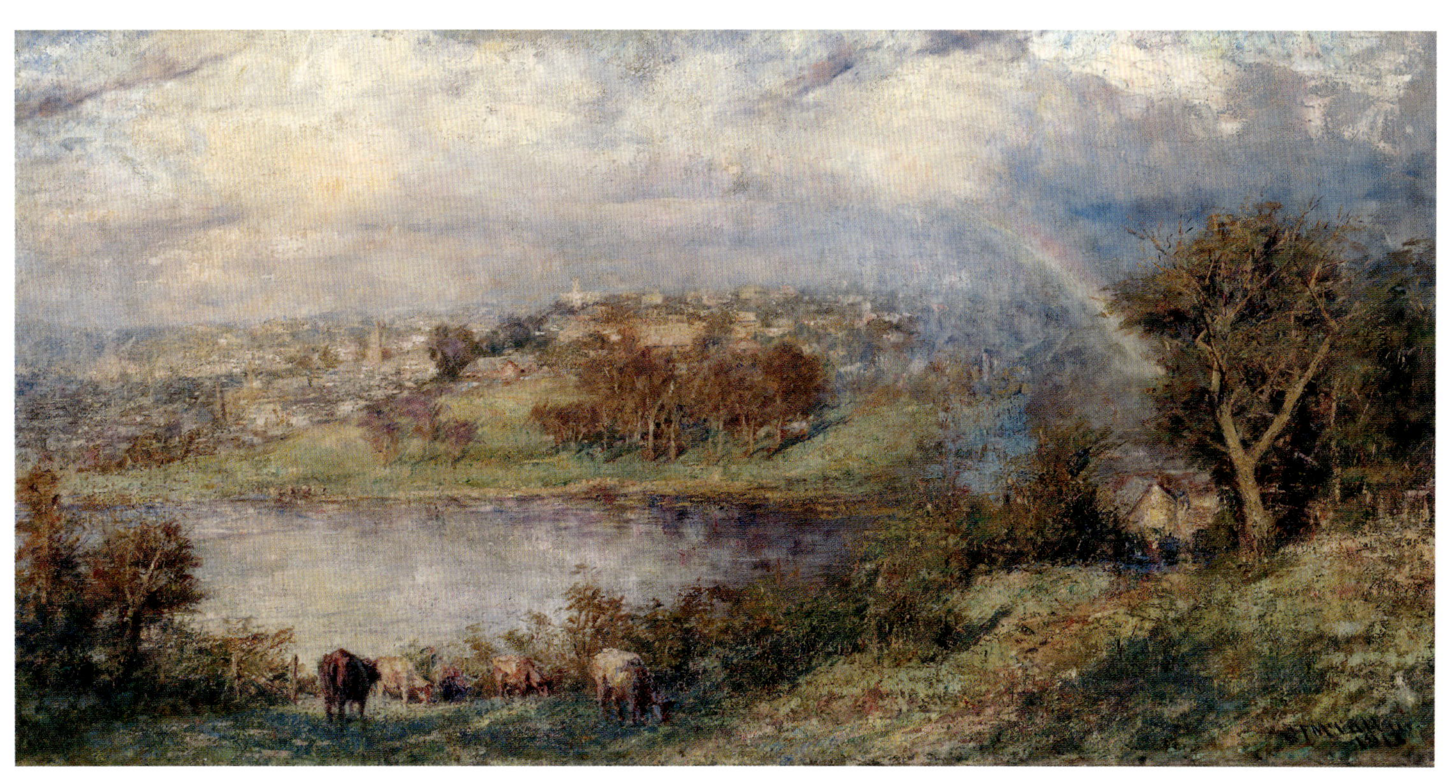

W. LISTER LISTER

born Australia 1859 died Australia 1943
England, France 1867–88
Federal Capital site 1913
painted in Sydney
oil on canvas, 159 x 284 cm
Australian Parliament House, Canberra, Historic Memorials Collection, purchased 1913

On the advice, of the art advisory board, it has been provided in the terms and conditions of the commission that the painting must be a panoramic picture 6 ft. by 4 ft., and be correct in regard to the geographical features of the landscape in every respect. A midday effect is preferred … Delivery must be made during the last week of June, 1913. The competition will be confined to Australian artists in the various States.
(*Advertiser*, 19 December 1912)

Early in the year the Federal Government decided to secure for the Federal Parliament House, when it is established, a painting of the site where the capital will stand as it was when a commencement was made with the work of building the city. Accordingly, the Cabinet invited artists to send in pictures, and it was announced that the picture chosen would be bought for £250.
(*Sydney Morning Herald*, 12 July 1913)

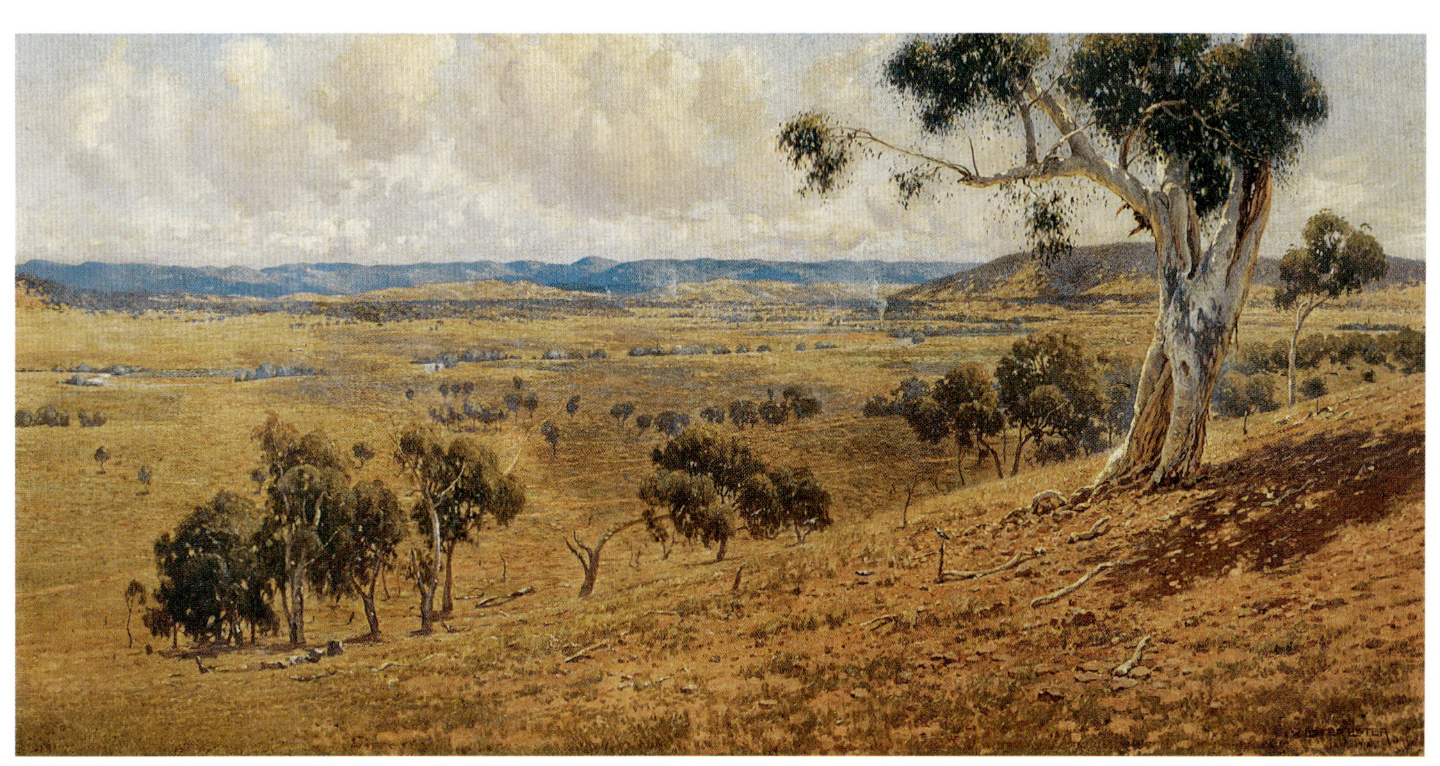

PENLEIGH BOYD

born England 1890 died Australia 1923
Australia from 1894; England 1911–13
The Federal Capital site 1913
painted in Melbourne
oil on canvas, 151 x 274 cm
Australian Parliament House, Canberra, Historic Memorials Collection, purchased 1913

*The art advisory board, consisting of representatives from each State, with Mr. Hugh
Paterson as chairman, was appointed to consider the merits of the pictures submitted,
and on Wednesday last they reduced the dozen entrants to two. To-day further consideration
was given to the matter, and it was eventually decided to purchase the work of Mr. W. Lister
Lister, of Sydney. Second place was secured by Mr. Penley [sic] Boyd, of Melbourne. The board
has advised the Government to secure this painting also …*
(*Sydney Morning Herald*, 12 July 1913)

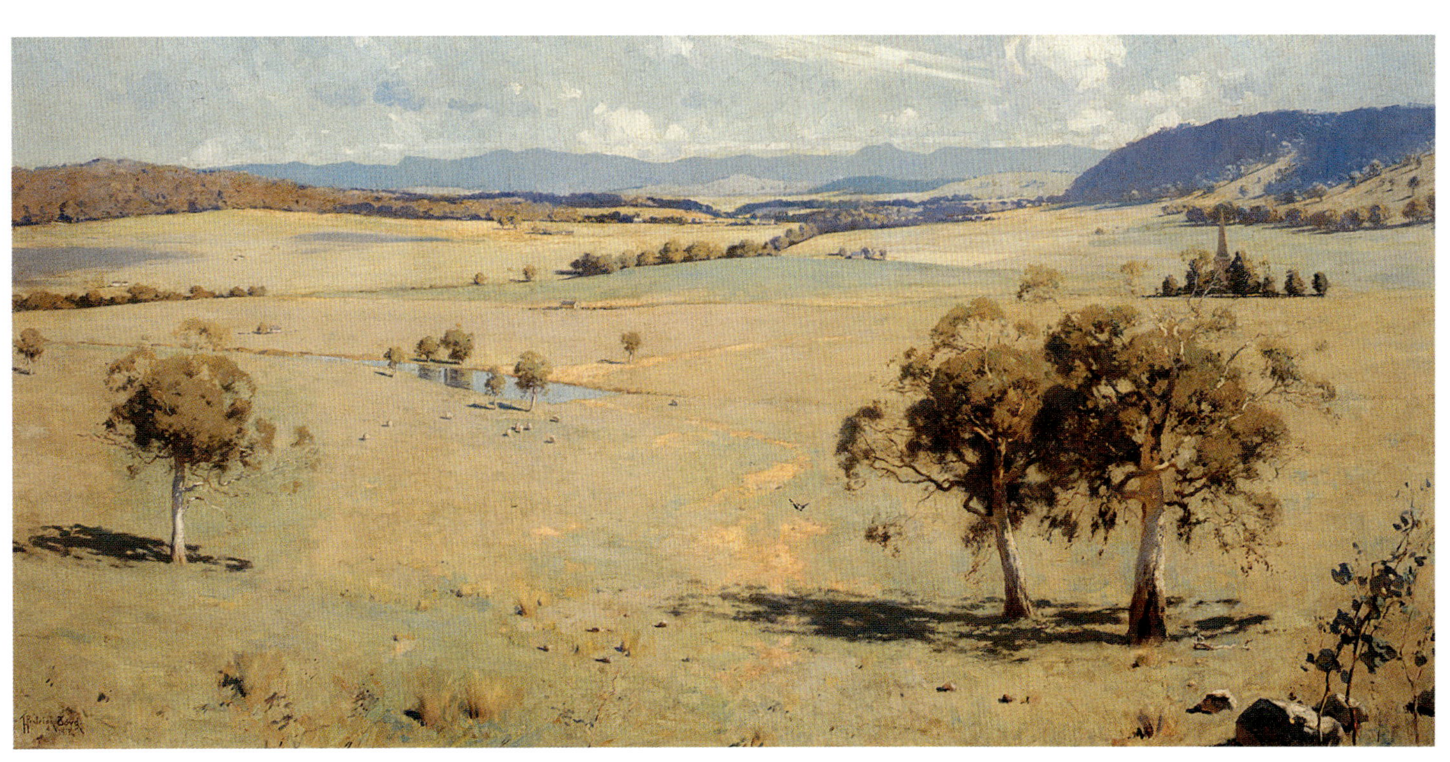

born England 1890 died Australia 1923
Australia from 1894; England 1911–13
Bridge and wattle at Warrandyte 1914
painted in Warrandyte, Victoria
oil on canvas, 91.5 x 137 cm
National Gallery of Australia, Canberra, purchased 1971

Wattle.
Yell'd figures we wait in the slumbering land.
Till Spring plucks the veil with a radiant hand.
Wattle by Geraldine Rede 1909[12]

Bridge and wattle, Warrandyte announces its Australian identity by titular association with the luminous yellow bloom, and complementary palette of warm golden and green tones. Wattle was formalised as a national floral symbol when it was entwined through the coat of arms in 1912 and wattle day sanctioned by the Governor-General in 1992 and now held annually on 1 September. Penleigh Boyd may even have seen wattle available for home-sick expatriates in Selfridges in London when he visited England in 1912.

Boyd was a student in Melbourne for the majority of the Federation era. Travelling to Europe in 1911, Boyd had met E. Phillips Fox and Ethel Carrick in Paris, and was inspired by Fox's impressionist approach. On his return to Australia in 1912 he turned his attention to the light and colours of the Australian landscape. *Bridge and wattle at Warrandyte* 1914, was painted in the bushland outside Melbourne, known for its wattle groves, to which a number of artists were drawn over the subsequent decades.

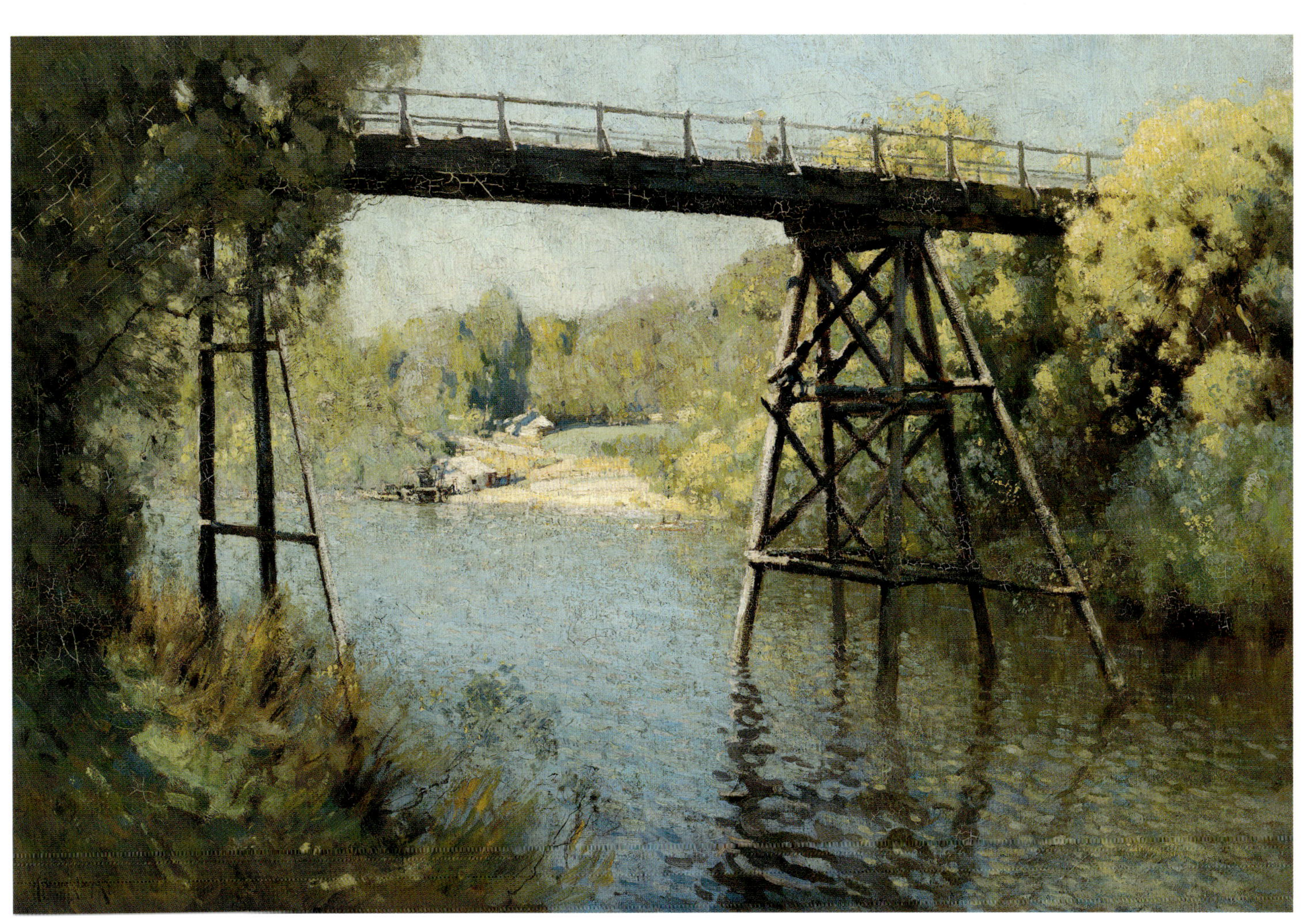

born Australia 1889 died United States of America 1959
United States of America from 1938
The woodcutter 1914
painted in Eltham, Victoria
oil on board, 45.5 x 35.5 cm
National Gallery of Australia, Canberra, purchased 2011

Under clear cold stars their camp fire had been lighted. On the edge of odorous eucalyptus forests, their broad axes had flashed in the sunlight.
(Edwin J. Brady, *Australia unlimited*, 1918)

The Australian bush labourer in Federation paintings possessed strength, masculinity and a rough, yet unassuming heroism; qualities romanticised as typical of the bush character at the time.

Painted near Eltham in Victoria, *The woodcutter* is late in the context of Federation art, but early in Percy Leason's career. Leason was distinctly anti-modern in his approach to painting when he created this picture, and here suggests nostalgia for the passing of an era of labouring by hand on the farm and in the forest as rural industries became increasingly mechanised.

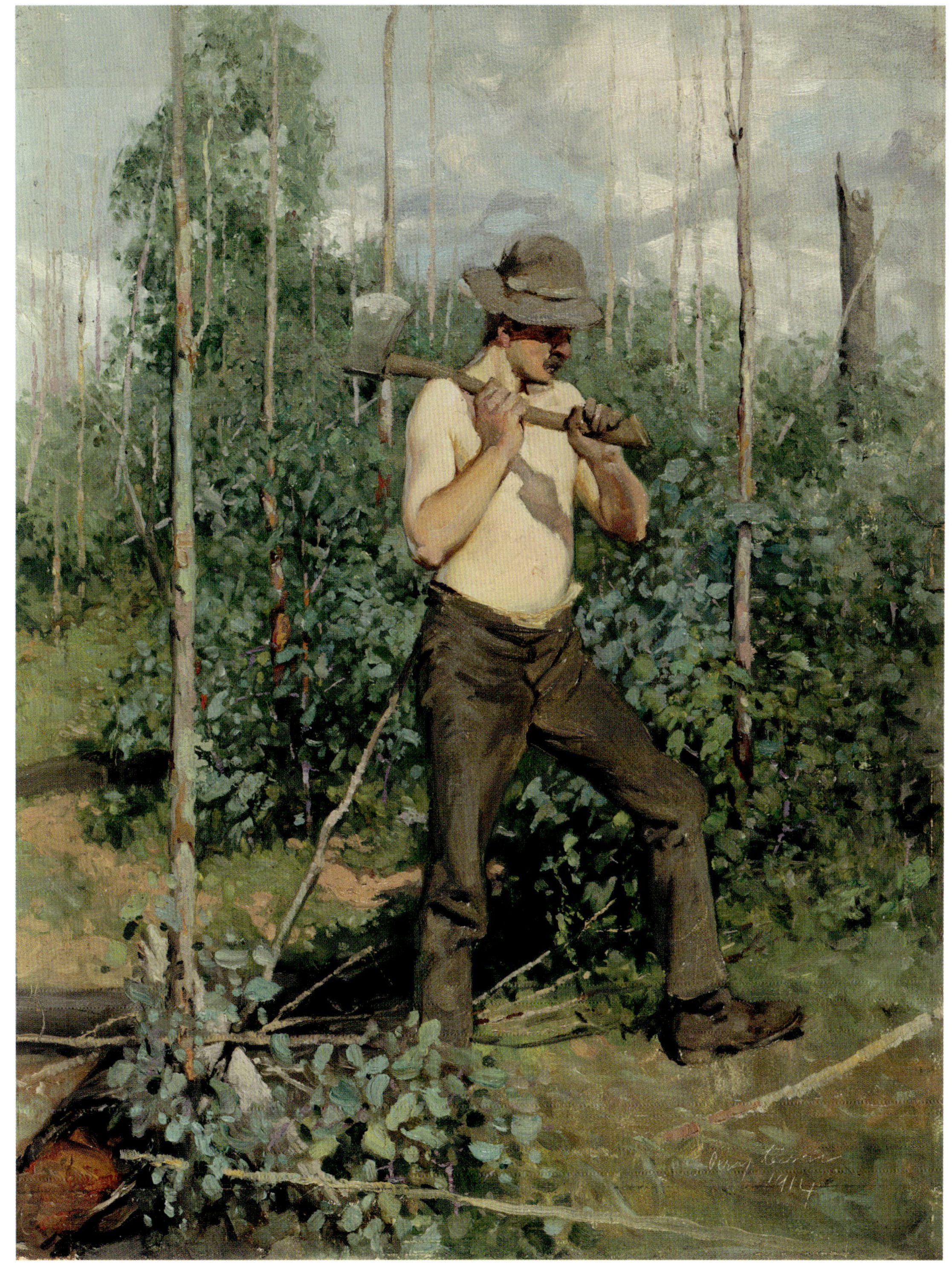

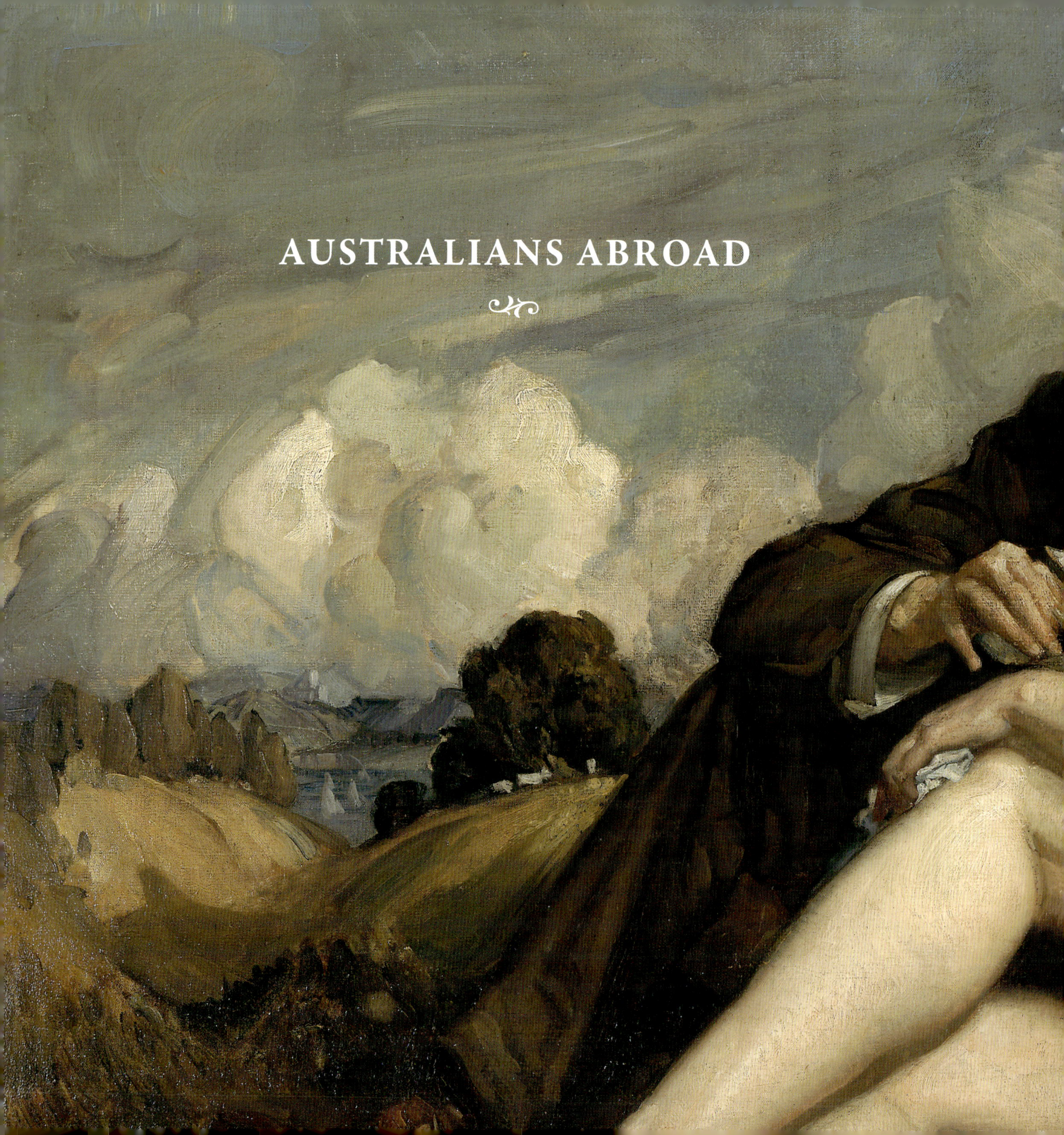
AUSTRALIANS ABROAD

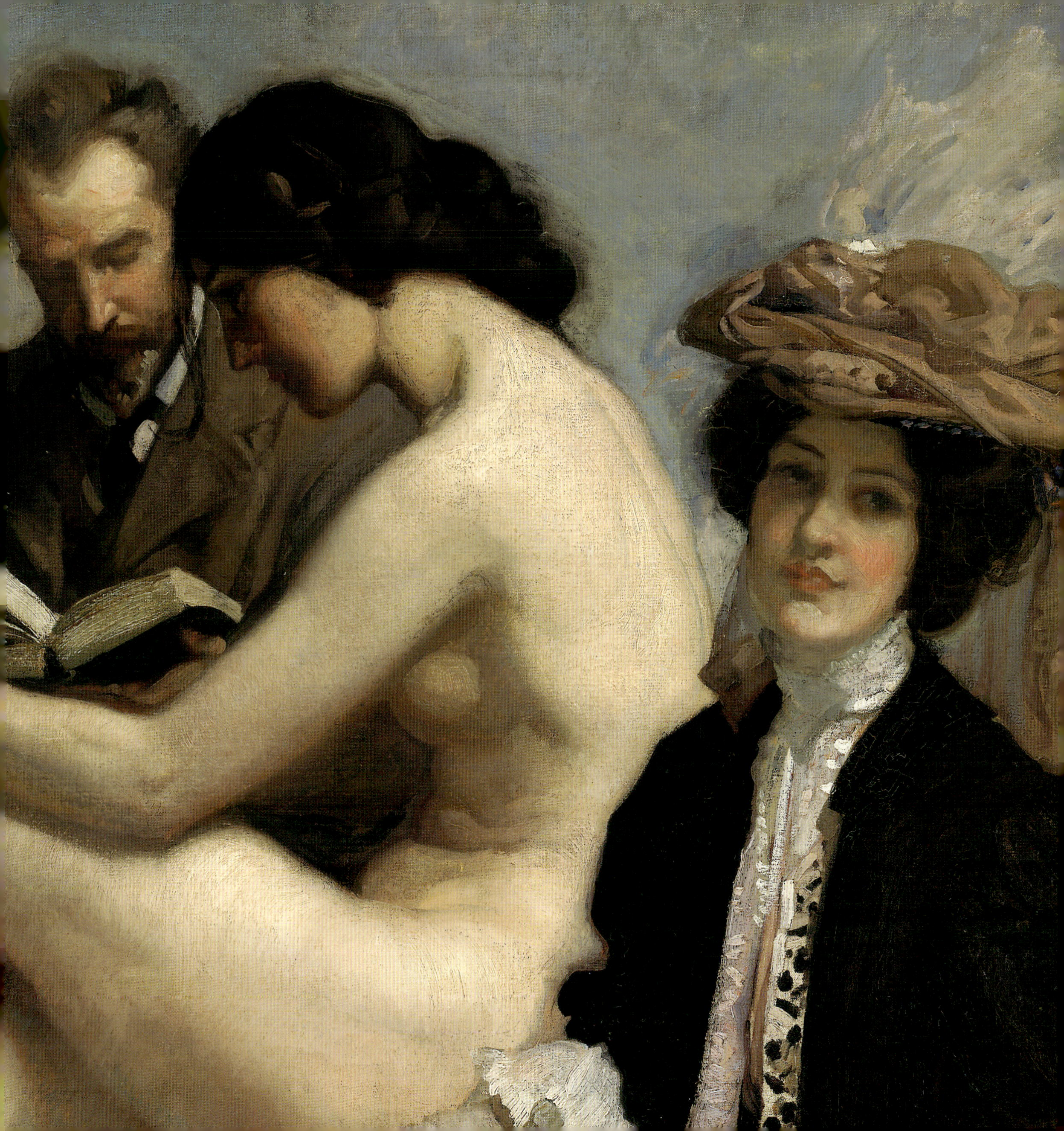

born Scotland 1877 died Australia 1906
Australia from 1878; England, France 1900–02
A mountain shepherd (An Italian dwarf) 1901
painted in Paris
oil on canvas, 167.5 x 110.8 cm
National Gallery of Australia, Canberra, gift of Nell Fullerton, niece of the artist,
in memory of her parents, Sir John and Lady Ramsay 1980

While painting *A mountain shepherd (An Italian dwarf)* Hugh Ramsay wrote to his brother Harry Ramsay about the experience (24 October 1901):

> I am painting a brigand or something. Supposed to be an Italian Mountain Shepherd, but looks more like a gnome or hobgoblin. He's a little nuggetty dwarflike fierce little cuss, so I keep me 'vervolver' in my hip pocket ready. It's awfully interesting both the man and the costume.

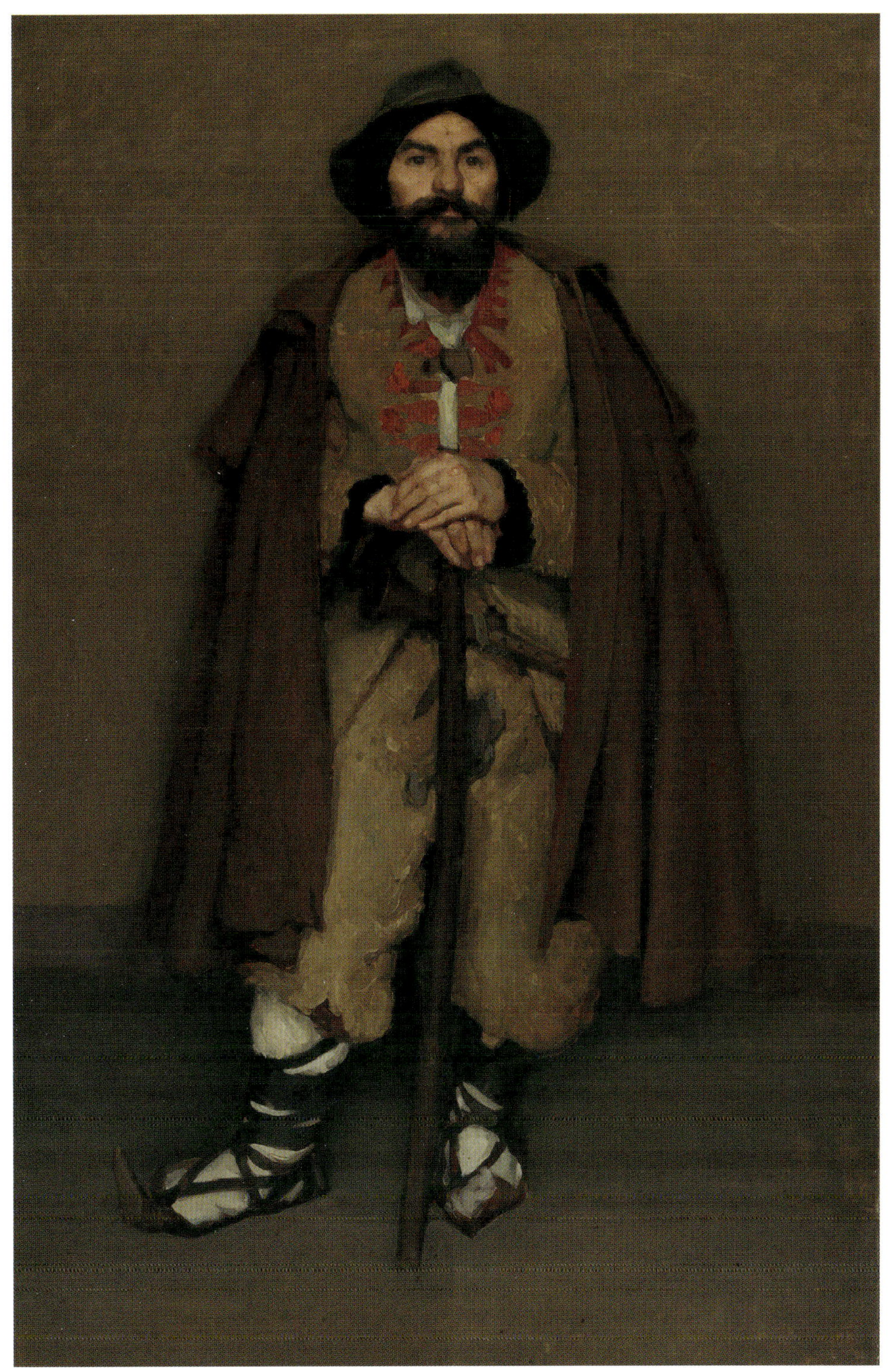

HUGH RAMSAY

born Scotland 1877 died Australia 1906
Australia from 1878; England, France 1900–02
Paris rooftops 1901
painted in Paris
oil on canvas,
National Gallery of Australia, Canberra, purchased 2011

Hugh Ramsay wrote copious letters home from his Paris studio between 1900 and 1902 of the delights and challenges he faced living away from home for the first time. The first extract is taken from a letter to his brother Harry Ramsay (2 May 1901); the second is from a letter to his father (28 March 1902).

> The Grand Vernissage was on the Tuesday, and the place was packed full of fashionables, so that you couldn't look at pictures for fear of getting on some duchess's train … You can't imagine the size of the exhibitions, the New and Old Salons. It's terrific. They're both held in the big Grand Palais de[s] Beaux Arts, a most magnificent building, by the Seine, opposite the Eiffel Tour [*sic*]…

> I've got some grand news for you this time. I've had 4 pictures accepted by the Salon. Just fancy 4 when one would have made me lucky and quite content. It's rather an extraordinary thing, so I'm told, as they seldom accept more than two, even from experienced and recognised men, let alone a young fellow like myself, practically exhibiting for the first time … Of course Paris is a hard place for money making, although it's the best working art centre in the world. To go to London with a good Salon record, however, will be of great importance to me.

Tragically, Ramsay's life was cut short at the age of twenty nine. He returned to Australia in 1903 to recover from tuberculosis, brought about by cold Parisian winters with inadequate clothing, heating or funds to buy enough food, and died three years later in Melbourne.

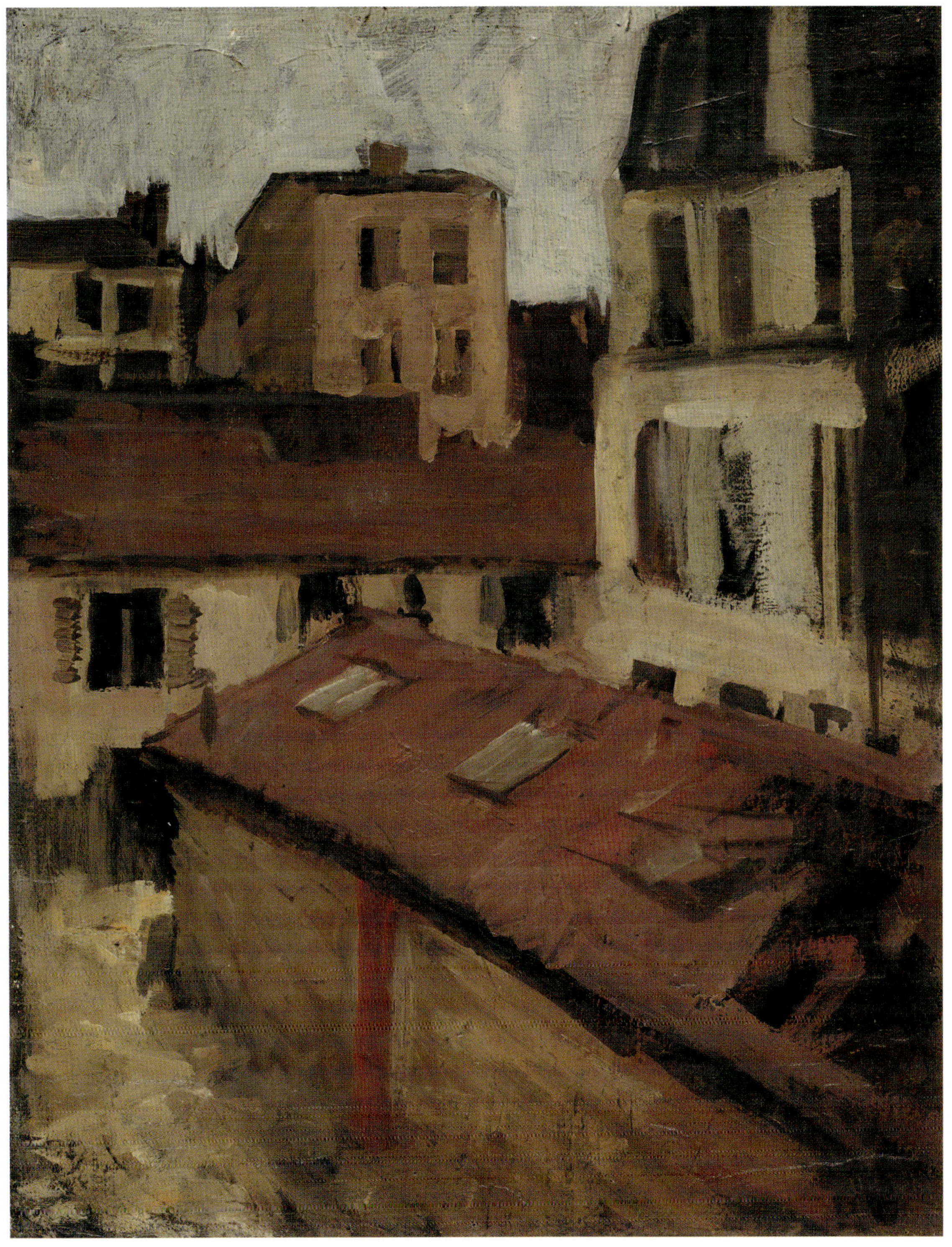

born Germany 1877 died Australia 1968
Australia from 1884; Europe, England 1899–1903
On the Marne at Charenton 1901
painted in Paris
oil on canvas mounted on composition board, 15.3 x 21 cm
National Gallery of Australia, Canberra, purchased 2010

With the financial support of four South Australian businessmen, Hans Heysen studied in Europe from 1899 to the end of 1903. To ensure short-term returns for their support and fostering the longer-term potential of Heysen's talent, the investors signed an agreement in October 1899, including terms such as:

> During the currency of this agreement the said Hans Heysen shall and will once in every month at least by letter addressed to the said William Laidlaw Davidson communicate a full and complete report of his progress and movements and of the work which he has for the month immediately preceding each such report been engaged upon and of the monies expended by him with the details of such expenditure.[13]

Heysen stuck to the agreement closely, and managed his stipend carefully to stretch out his time abroad for as long as possible.

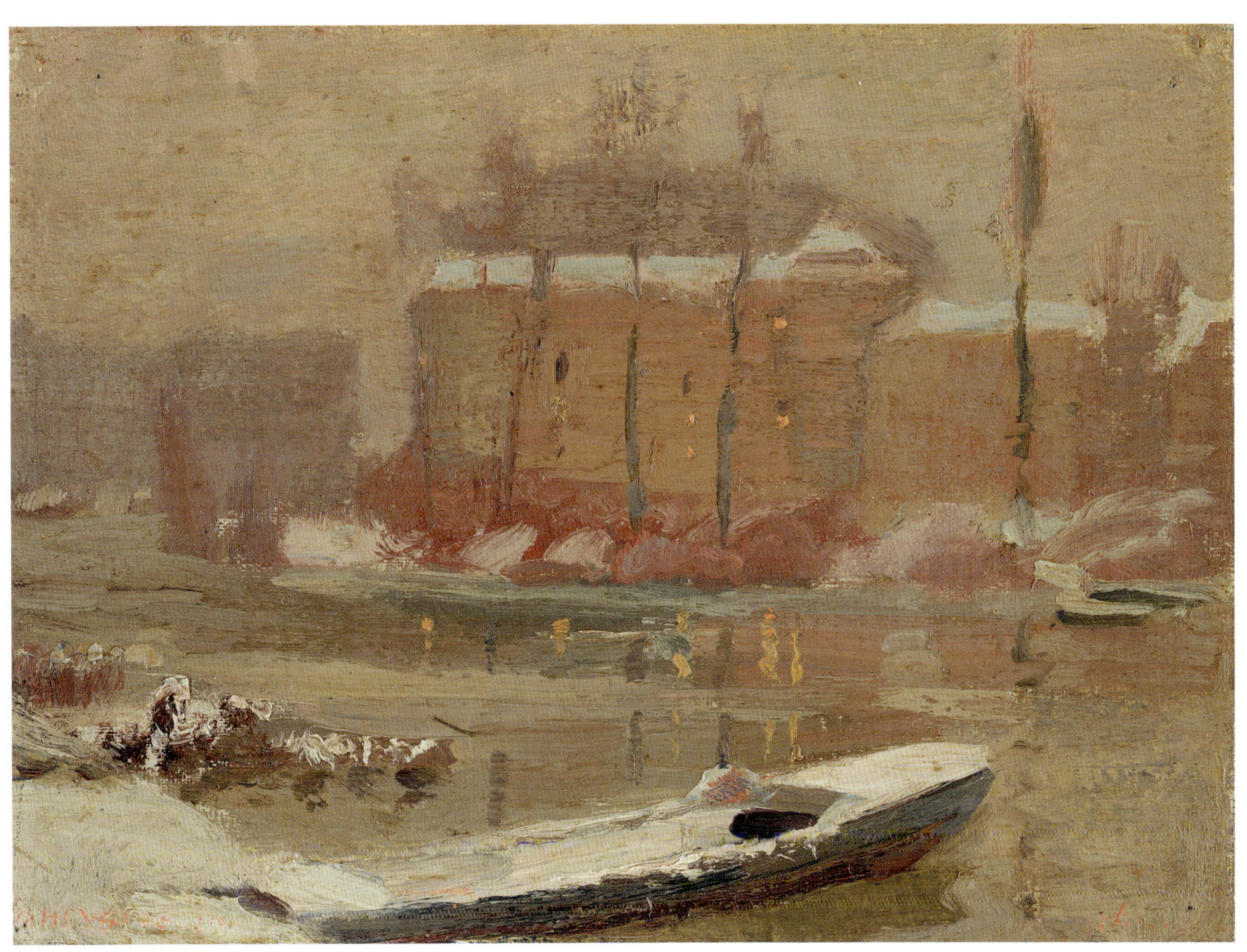

born Germany 1877 died Australia 1968
Australia from 1884; Europe, England 1899–1903
From the studio window, Paris c .1902
painted in Paris
oil on canvas mounted on composition board, 14.3 x 20.2 cm
National Gallery of Australia, Canberra, purchased 2010

*After a sojourn of four years in the art centres of the old world Mr. Hans Heysen has
returned to the city of his adoption. Mr. Heysen is one of the fortunate few who are gifted by
Nature with that rare combination of talents – the faculties of perception and of execution.
Questioned by his interviewer regarding his four years' travels, Mr. Heysen showed clearly
that the period was one of hard work. Morning, noon, and night seem to have been devoted
to the pursuit of that knowledge without which the artist's ambition cannot be realized.
Four winter sessions were spent in Paris, where drawing was studied in the mornings at the
Académie Julian under Jean Paul Laurens, and that notable professor Benjamin Constant.*
(*Register*, 7 October 1903)

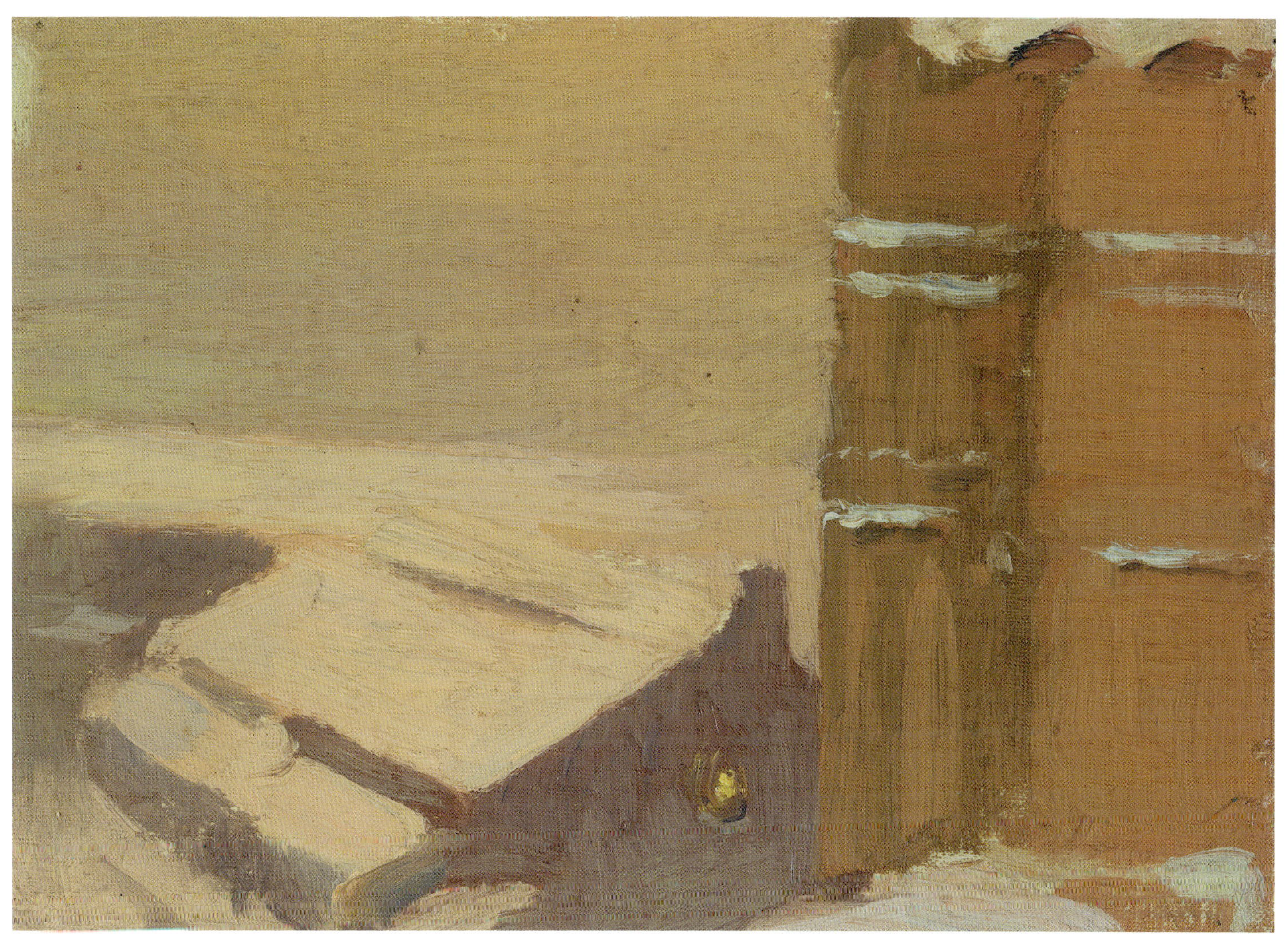

born Scotland 1877 died Australia 1906
Australia from 1878; England, France 1900–02
Self-portrait c. 1902
painted in Paris
oil on canvas, 45.8 x 40.4 cm
National Gallery of Australia, Canberra, purchased 1965

Life models were an expense that Hugh Ramsay, like many expatriate artists, could not often afford outside their classes at the various Académies – Delécluze, Colarossi or Julian. To quench his voracious desire to paint and experiment at every opportunity, Ramsay depicted himself over and over again.

Self-portrait c. 1902 is one of more than twenty-five self-portraits painted by Ramsay over a period of three years. His bravura brush work reveals his growing admiration for the work of American painter John Singer Sargent.

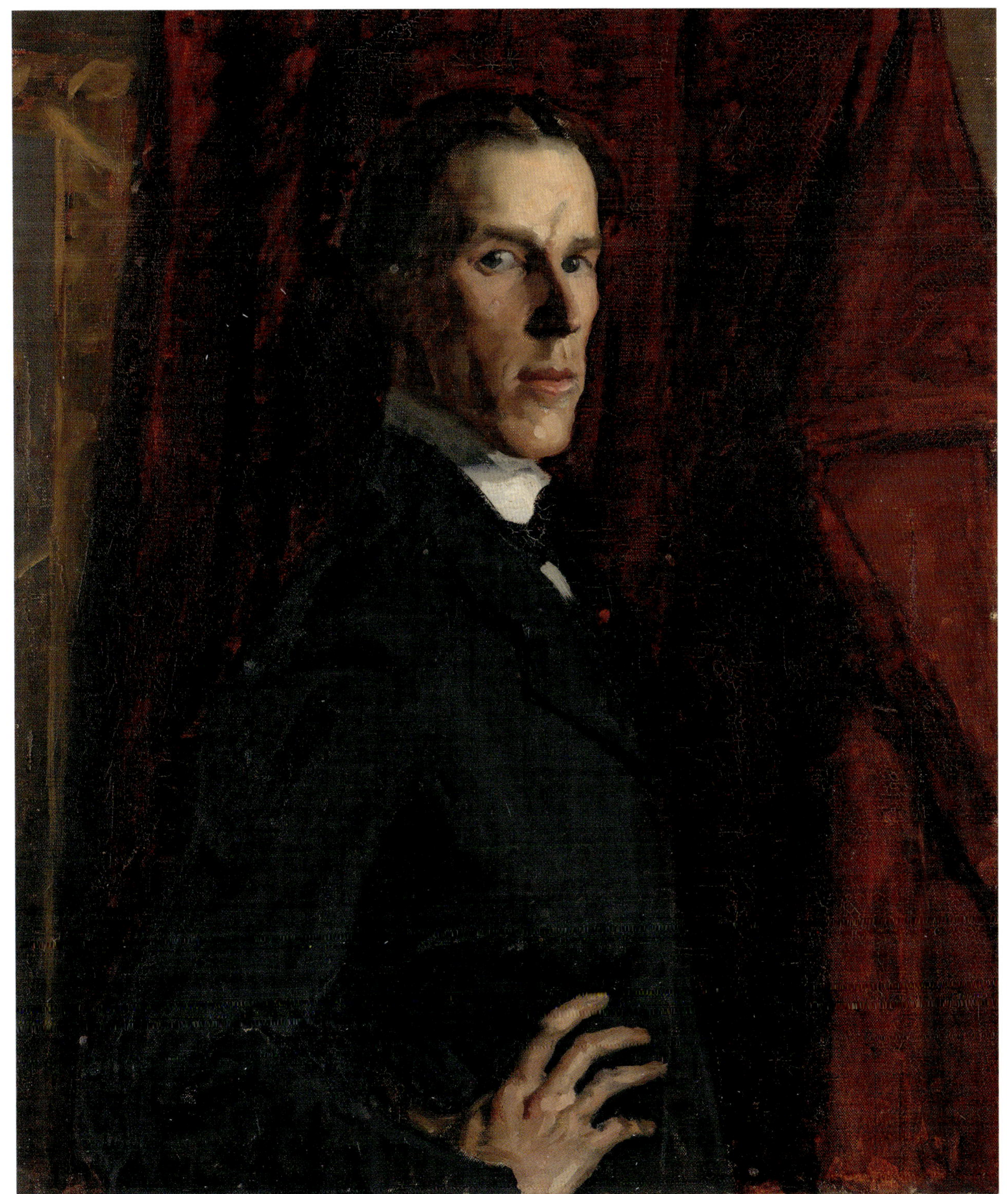

born Australia 1865 died Australia 1915
Europe, England 1887–92; England, Europe 1901–13
Elsie, daughter of H.W. Brooks, Esquire 1904
painted in London
oil on canvas, 136.5 x 71.3 cm
National Gallery of Australia, Canberra, purchased 1963

At the door of the Royal Academy, he [E. Phillips Fox] says, an artist must knock two or three times, and knock hard. There is no distinction in getting a picture into the R. A. … But it is necessary for a portrait painter to exhibit in the R.A. Fox tells the yarn of an artist who was commissioned by a man to do a portrait of his wife for £100. He added 'I'll make it £500 if you get it into the Academy' … [T]hough the Academy is especially a people's show, the artist who aims to be an Academician must make an artistic and not a popular success.
(*Bulletin*, Red Page, 21 May 1908)

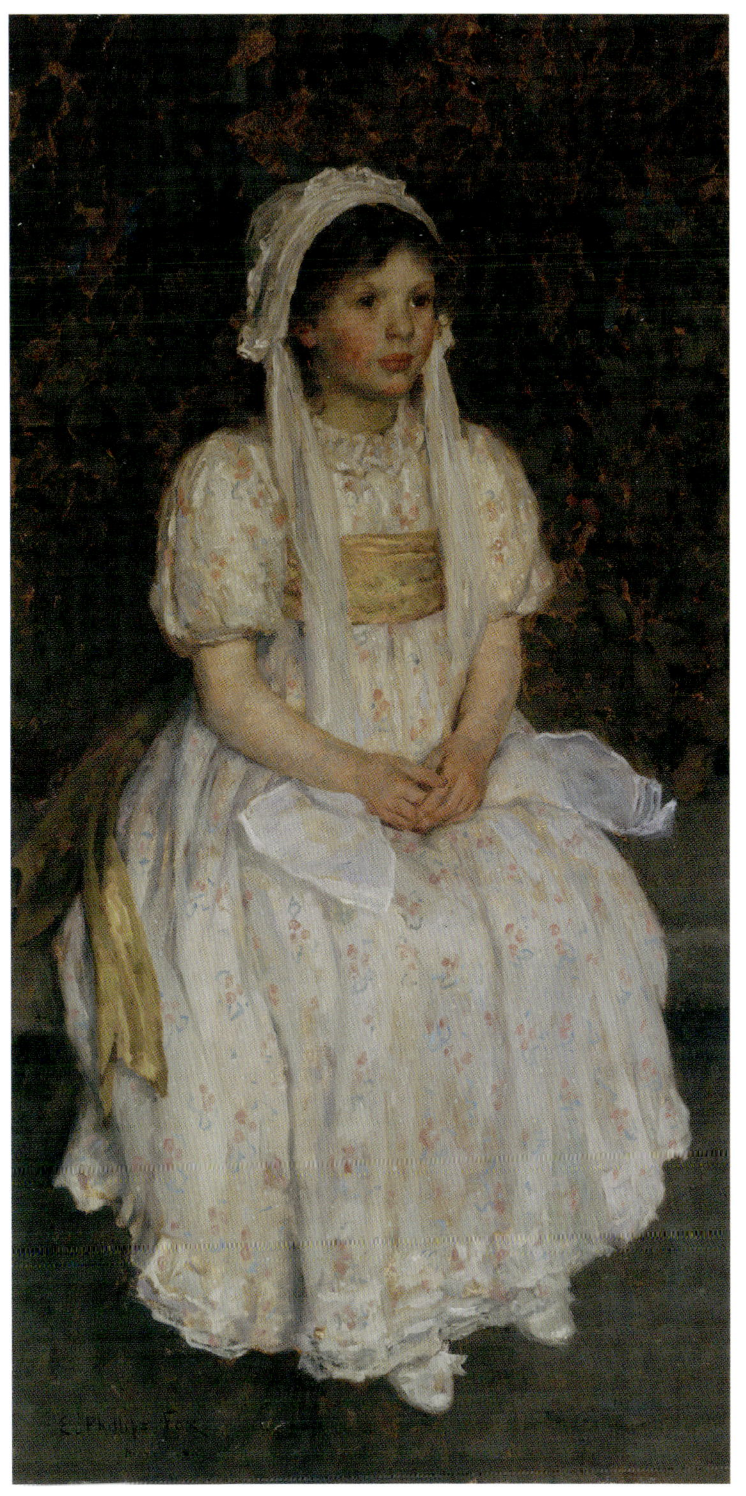

ARTHUR STREETON

born Australia 1867 died Australia 1943
England 1897–1906, 1907–24
Kent harvest c. 1904
painted in Kent, England
oil on wood panel, 18.5 x 24.1 cm
National Gallery of Australia, Canberra, bequest of Mary Meyer in memory of her
husband Dr Felix Meyer 1975

Pastoral regions in Sussex, Surrey, Essex and Kent proved a magnet to Streeton over
six summers between 1898 and 1906. In 1904, staying close to the town of Hayes,
in Kent, he painted harvesting scenes, attracted to the stacks of new mown hay
and cloud formations.[14]

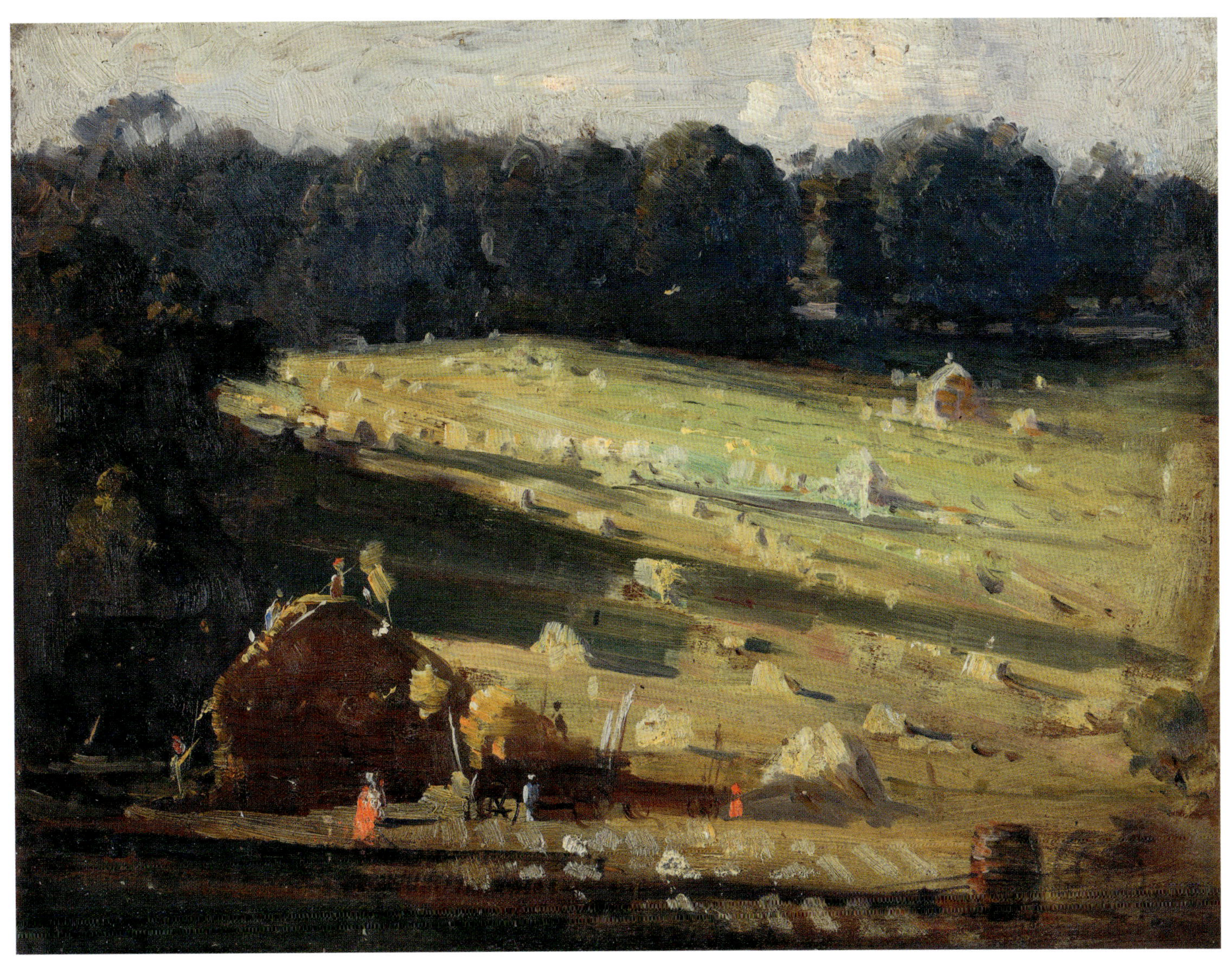

born Australia 1867 died Australia 1943
England 1897–1906, 1907–24
View of Hampstead Heath from Jack Straw's Castle c. 1901–08
Hampstead Heath, London
oil on canvas, 35.5 x 45.9 cm
National Gallery of Australia, Canberra, bequest of Mary Meyer in memory of her
husband Dr Felix Meyer 1975

'Working from 'Jack Straws Castle' toward Harrow – you know the view', Streeton
wrote to Tom Roberts (14 February 1901), 'it's like looking over the sea …'[15]

The rolling slopes of Hampstead Heath, on the outskirts of London, comprise almost
325 hectares of preserved semi-wild landscape. The Heath was depicted by English
Romantic painter John Constable, and inspired Arthur Streeton's numerous visits
to the region between 1901 and 1908.

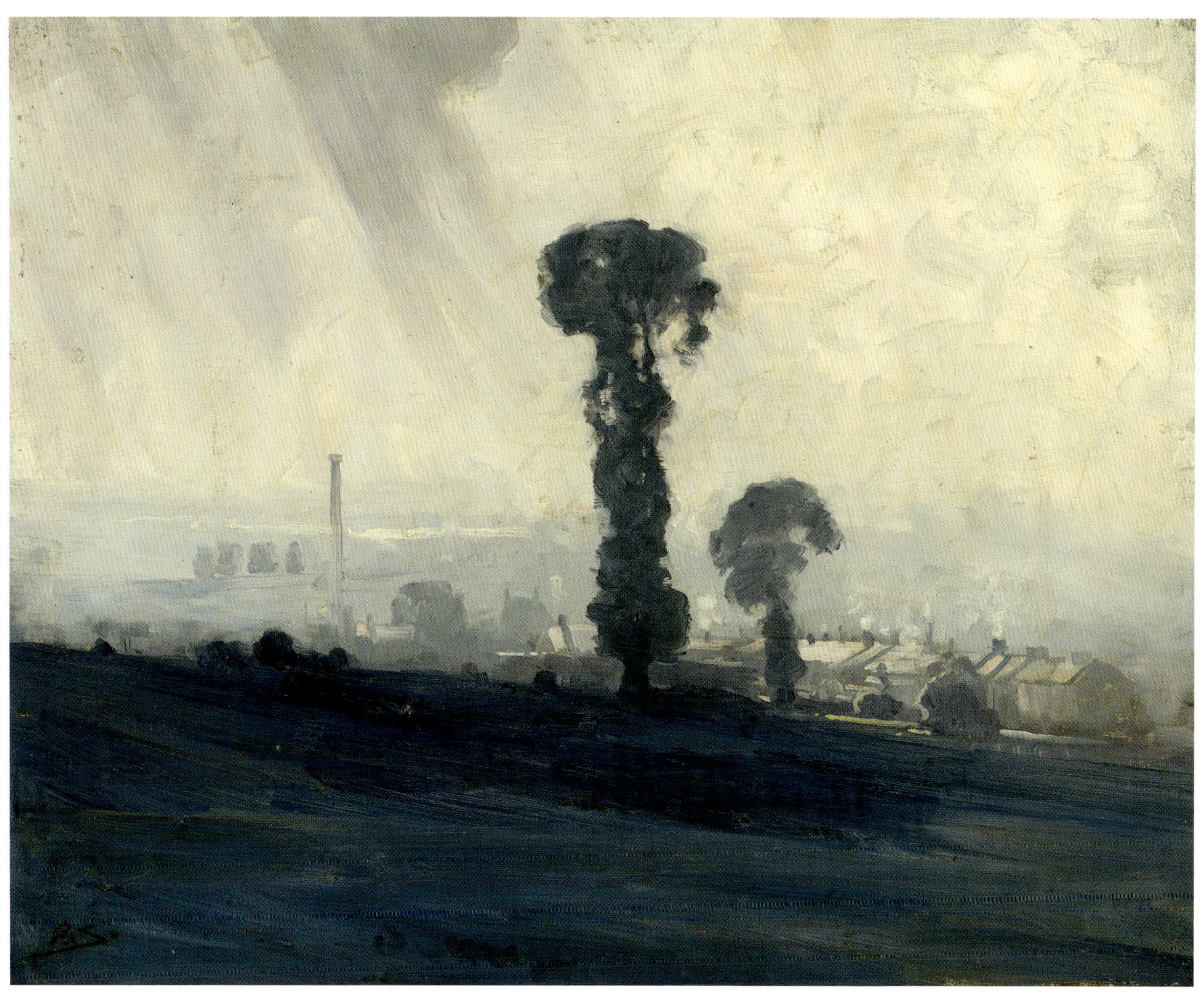

born Russia 1873 died Australia 1930
Australia 1887–1900, and from 1921; Europe 1900–21
The sonnet c. 1907
painted in London
oil on canvas, 113.3 x 177.4 cm
National Gallery of Australia, Canberra, bequest of John B. Pye 1963

Well, G.W. Lambert … is forging ahead faster than anyone from Australia. His work is beginning to attract attention, and he has turned out some splendid portraits. You are going to hear a good deal of Lambert …

So said Arthur Streeton in an interview with the *Sydney Morning Herald* (31 December 1906) while visiting Australia from London in 1906. Streeton confirmed George W. Lambert's standing among his Australian and British colleagues in London, noting the benefit of exposure to European art, and Lambert's stamp of originality.

… what he has seen has done him good. He has seen it with Lambert's eyes worked from it with Lambert's hands, and the personality of Lambert is on everything he does … His force, I think; although you can't put into words exactly what makes it appeal to you. It was Millais who said: 'What constitutes the finest art is indescribable – the drawing not faultless, but possessing some essence beyond what is sufficient. It's not how beautifully you use the gloves – it's how hard you hit.'

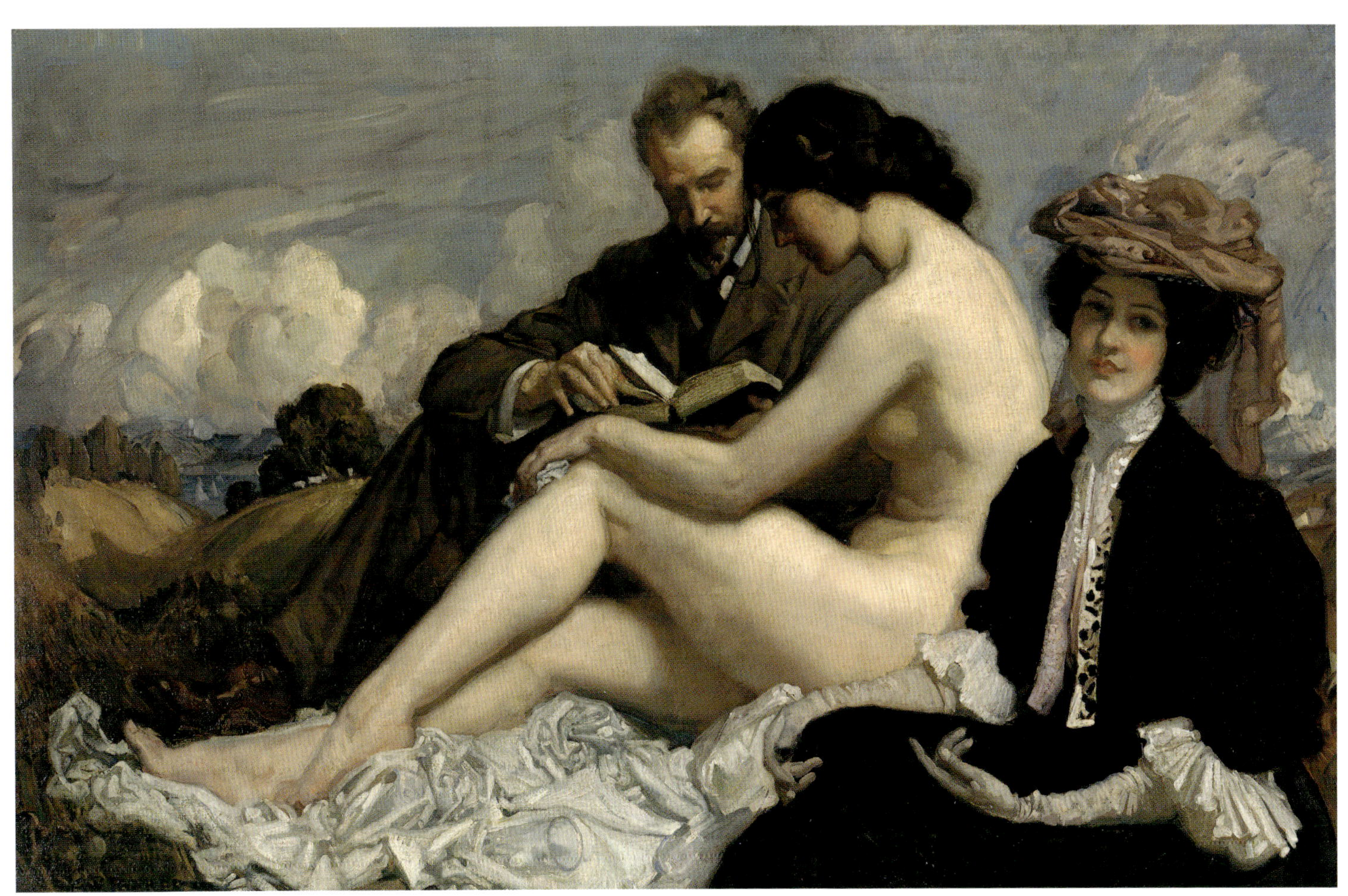

born Australia 1867 died Australia 1943
England 1897–1906, 1907–24
La Salute, from Riva Schiavoni c. 1908
painted in Venice
oil on canvas, 28.2 x 38.4 cm
National Gallery of Australia, Canberra, purchased 1959

In a letter to his illustrious friend, the collector, antrohropologist and museum
director, Baldwin Spencer (8 October 1908), Streeton wrote:

> Here we are again in this fascinating old city … while Mrs. S sat some yards off
> on a seat in the 'Florian Café' reading 'Great Expectations' I sat surrounded by
> a great mob of about 40. It was extremely hot with so much humanity like a wall
> around me … I've seen no one else tackle it here – But I pulled it off.[16]

Streeton honeymooned in Venice in May 1908. Inspired by the bold Mediterranean
light he returned in October that year, painting works such as the glistening
La Salute, from Riva Schiavoni c. 1908, a view from the Bridge of Sighs, looking across
the Grand Canal to the Dogana and Santa Maria della Salute.[17] There is a freshness
and confidence in his impressions of the oft-depicted water city, described in a British
review (*Observer*, 1908) as carrying 'conviction in every brush stroke'.

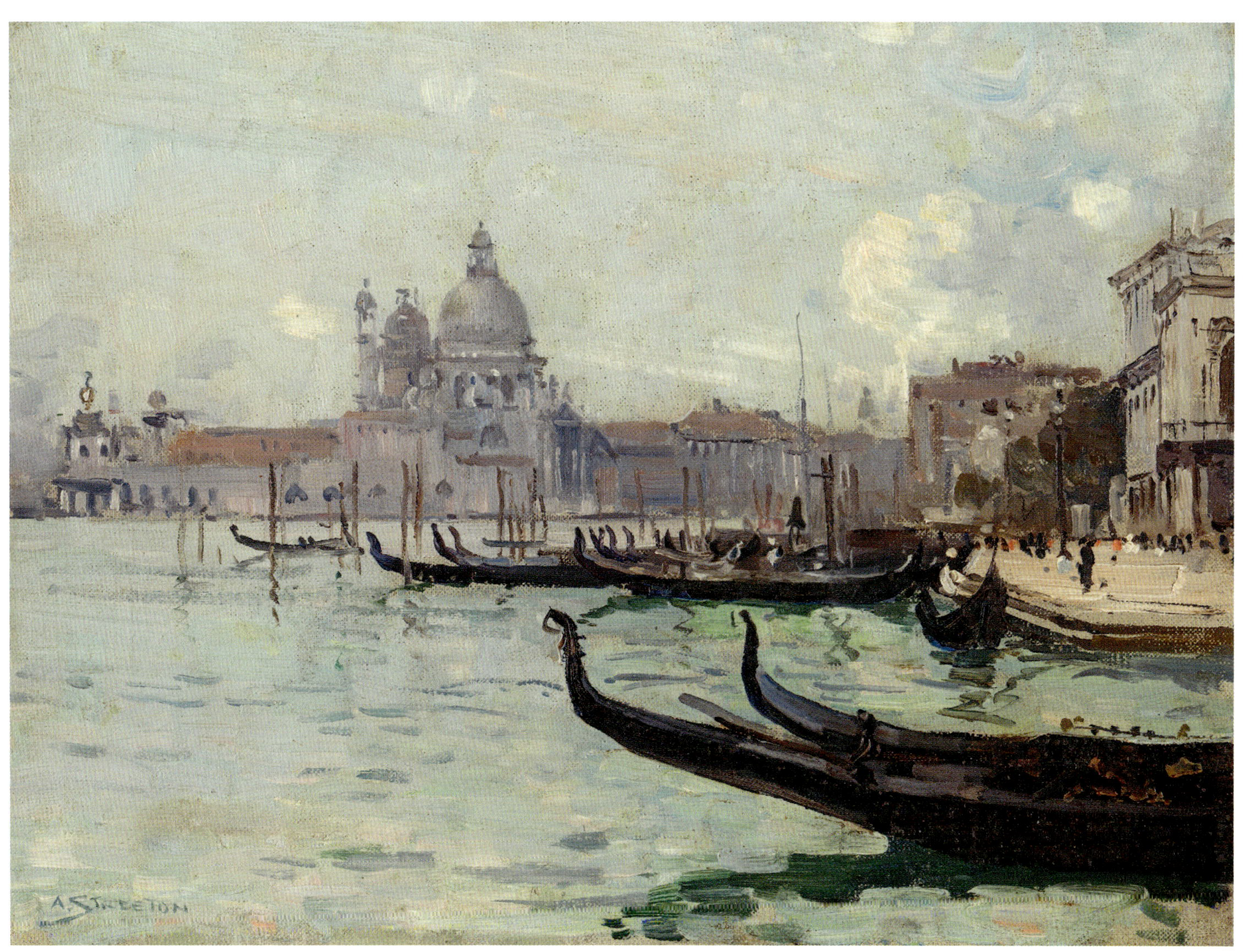

born Australia 1876 died United States of America 1958
England c. 1899–1911; United States of America from 1912
A haven beneath the hill, St Ives c. 1908
painted in St Ives, Cornwall, England
oil on canvas, 140.5 x 164.5 cm
National Gallery of Australia, Canberra, purchased 1968

The young South Australian artist, Mr. Hayley Lever, R.B.A., has been fortunate enough to have his large canvas 'The Haven Beneath the Hill', hung in the New Salon, National[e] de[s] Beaux Arts Paris. This is the eighth time he has attained this honour, and this latest work is said to be the best he has yet finished. The scene depicted on the 6-ft. canvas is bathed in morning light, looking over housetops and to the harbour, with the quay on the left, where the herring boats are going out to sea. In the distance trains are seen making to market with the catch. Such well known artists as Mr. East, A.R.A., Mr. Olsson, and Mr. Brown, A.R.A., say it is quite a new outlook on St. Ives, and Mr Lever's best effort.
(*Register*, 3 May 1909)

Born in Adelaide in 1876, Hayley-Lever studied at James Ashton's Norwood Art School. Ashton encouraged Hayley-Lever to travel to Europe to further his study. With family support he left for Europe in the late 1890s, settling in the English seaport town of St Ives in 1899 where he lived and worked until 1911.

St Ives attracted a steady influx of artists from the late 1800s, and by the turn of the century was a lively cosmopolitan arts hub. Australian painters including E. Phillips Fox and George Bell all spent time capturing the local landscape. Hayley-Lever was associated with the British Impressionists Julius Olsson and Algernon Talmage, and became friends with a number of American expatriates. He was encouraged to travel to the United States in 1912, establishing himself there for the remainder of his life.

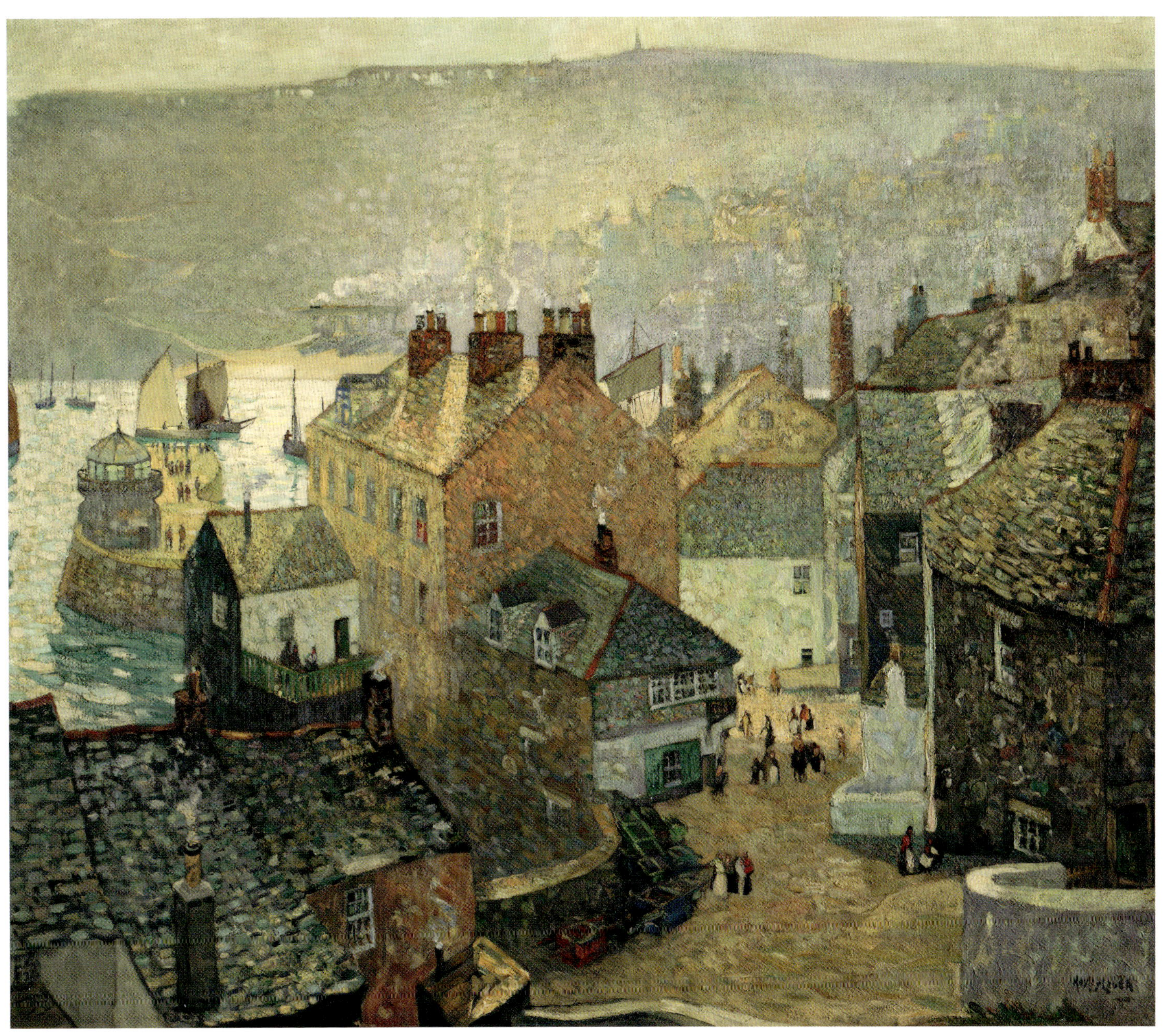

born Australia 1864 died Australia 1947
England 1884–86; France 1886–1933
Qui vient? [*Who comes?*] c. 1908
painted in Paris
oil on canvas, 81 x 54.2 cm
National Gallery of Australia, Canberra, bequest of John B. Pye 1963

'I agree with Tolstoi', Rupert Bunny stated in an interview with the *Sydney Morning Herald* (22 September 1911), during his first return visit to Australia since his departure in 1884. 'The aim of the artist should be the transmission of an emotion. He should paint only what appeals personally to himself. I do not believe in selecting extraordinary or unusual subjects. It is the quiet, everyday things that appeal to most people.'

On the coldest morning of the year Mr Rupert Bunny, a distinguished Victorian returned yesterday to his native land. Mr Bunny is better known in Paris than in Melbourne, for that is the way of Australia with her artists they must leave her to succeed. Mr Bunny has been away for 25 years, so long that he does not know any of the home-staying artists, so long that he slips occasionally into a French word for an English.
(*Argus*, 30 May 1911)

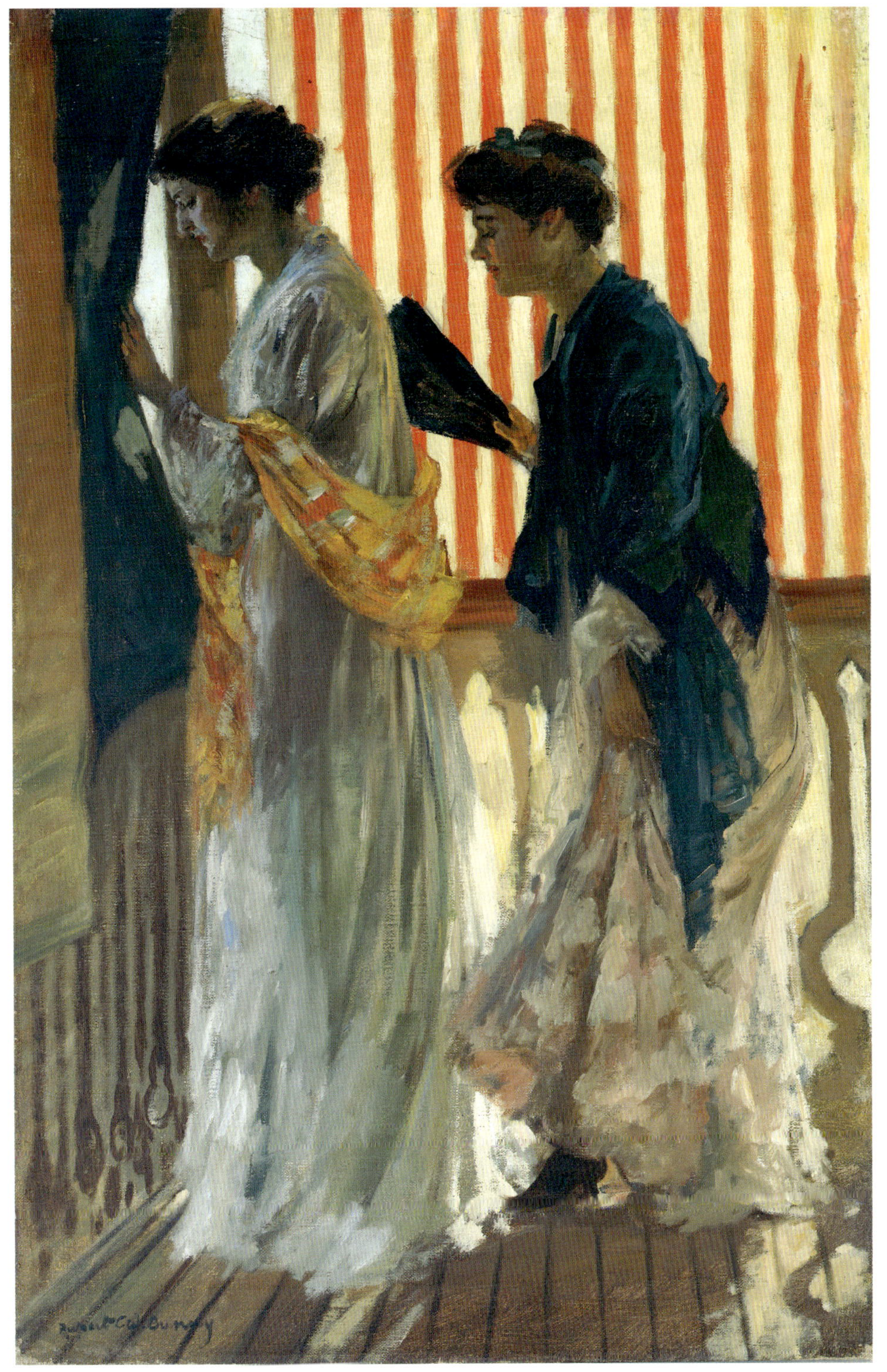

born Australia 1884 died Australia 1961
France, England 1907–18; France 1924–26
Snow, Montmartre c. 1912
painted in Paris
oil on canvas mounted on cardboard, 58.5 x 48.5 cm
National Gallery of Australia, Canberra, purchased 2008

She can paint pictures, with a brilliance, a mastery of composition, a sense of colour ranging
from the most subtle effects to a blaze of brilliance, a knowledge of drawing, a breadth of
handling, and a vigour of brushwork that are strangely masculine.
(*Daily Telegraph*, 11 June 1919)

'Women should be allowed to do everything they prove themselves capable of'
Hilda Rix Nicholas later stated, in an interview for the *Daily Telegraph* (9 June 1927).
'The work is the thing that matters, and not who does it.'

Hilda Rix Nicholas lived and worked abroad from 1907, producing a strong group
of figure studies and street scenes in cities from Paris to Tangier. The urban scene in
Snow, Montmartre is likely a view from Rix Nicholas's Paris studio. She exploits the
formal potential of the scene's intersecting rooftops, flattening the picture plane and
emphasising strong, simplified shapes. Her crisp, luminous, cool palette conveys
the stillness of winter, with long blue shadows emphasising the cold European light.
When Nicholas returned to Australia in 1918, she turned her focus to the bush,
creating distinctive nationalistic images of Australian rural life; a genre dominated
by her male peers.

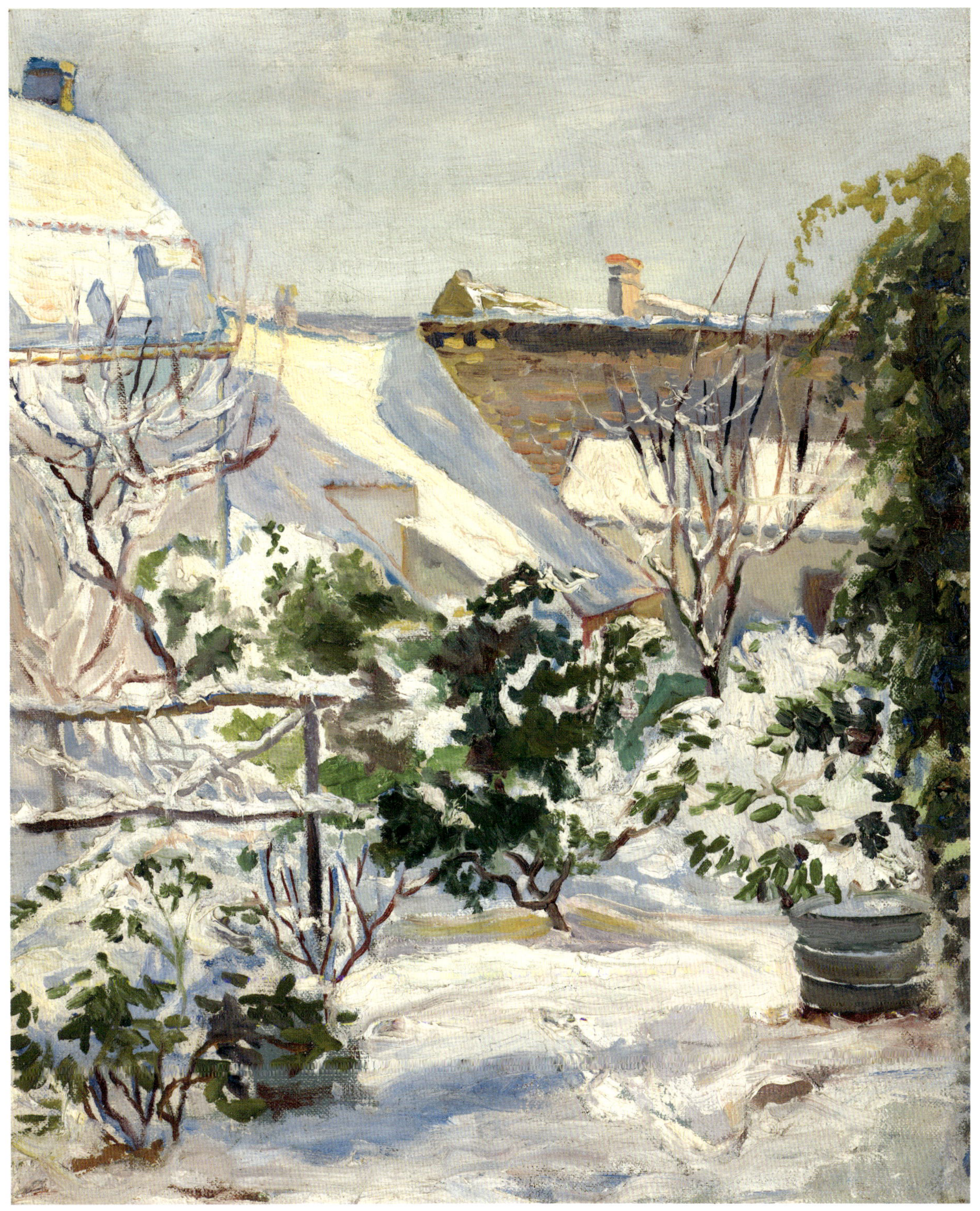

born Australia 1865 died Australia 1915
Europe, England 1887–92; England, Europe 1901–13
Promenade c. 1909
painted in Trouville, France
oil on wood panel, 26.6 x 35 cm
National Gallery of Australia, Canberra, purchased 1974

At the end of the European summer in which E. Phillips Fox painted *Promenade*, he wrote to his Australian friend Norman Carter (10 September 1909):

> I am still very much interested in plein air problems and have been working all this summer on studies for a couple of things I wish to paint in the winter … Have been going fairly strongly since our return from London where we went for a fortnight at Academy time … I think the Society business is bad for the English painters the French are more bohemian live more simply and put their whole effort into their work … We have had a wretched summer, no sunlight, most dissappointing [*sic*], especially when one has sunny motives [*sic*] on hand.[18]

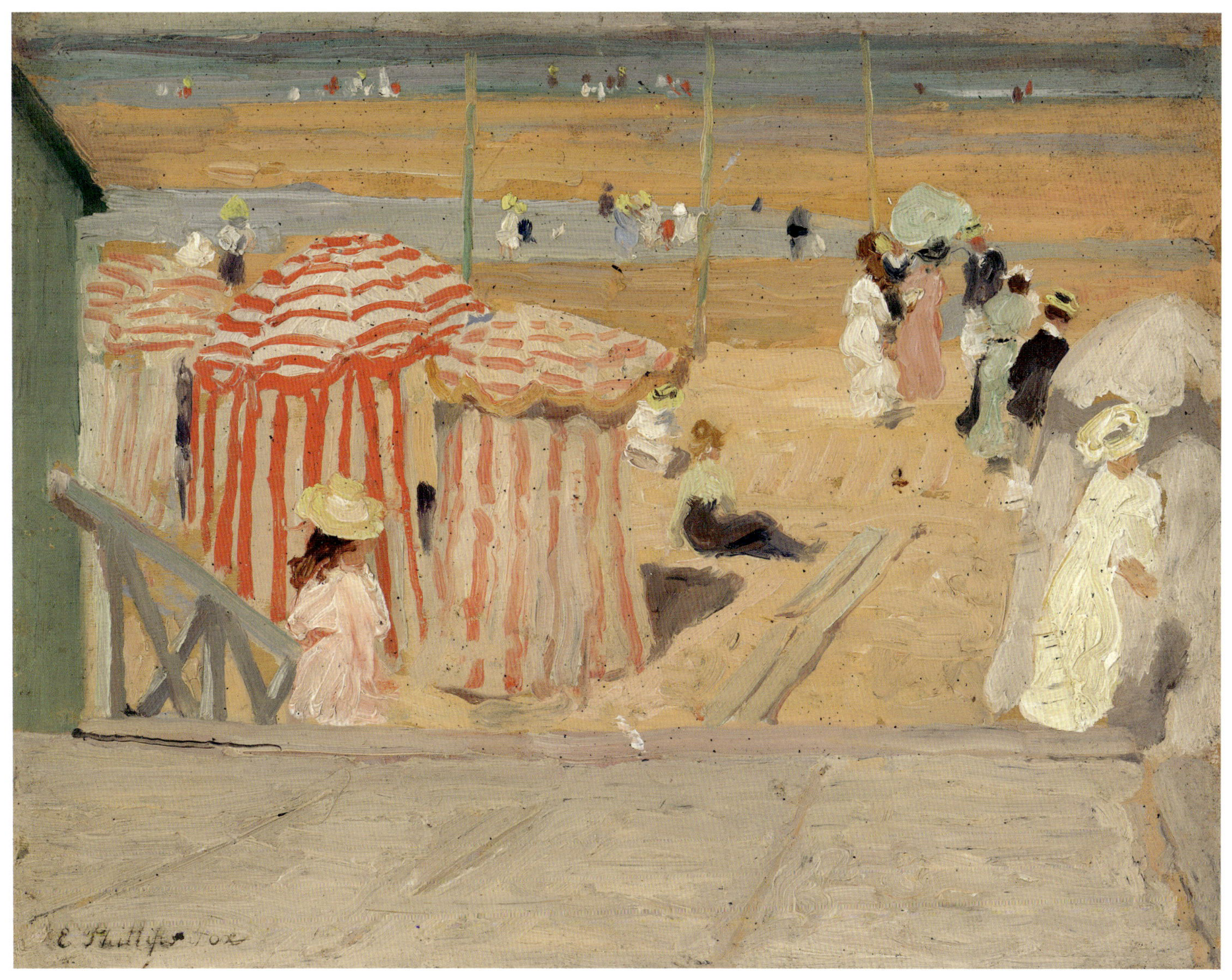

born England 1856 died Australia 1931
Australia from 1869; England, Europe 1881–85, 1903–23
Madame Hartl 1909–10
painted in London
oil on canvas, 114.5 x 76.6 cm
National Gallery of Australia, Canberra, purchased 1969

Tom Roberts wrote jubilantly to a friend in Melbourne in 1910 that:

> The portrait of Madame Ruby Hartl as La Tornabuoni is No.1 in the first room, just one above the line, and looks as well as it did in the studio … I couldn't have chosen a better place.[19]

His wife, Lillie Roberts, wrote to Lucy Simpson (28 October 1910) with mixed feelings about the great success of the portrait:

> Mrs Hartl too wants to buy her portrait, you know it was not a com[mission]. Tom wanted the opportunity of doing such a one & glad as we'll be of the money we'll be very sorry to lose her from the studio, she's a good example of my frames …[20]

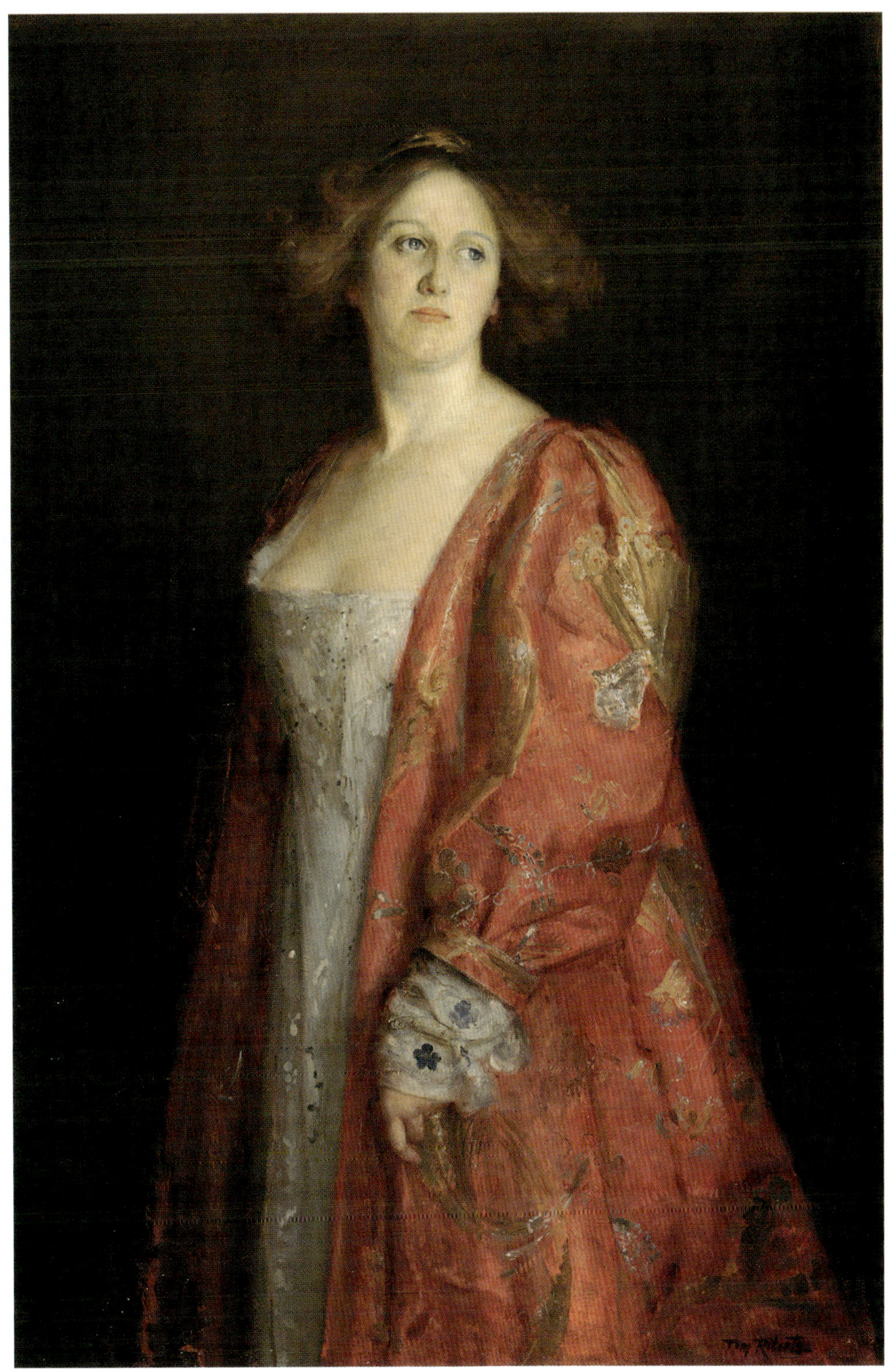

born Scotland 1875 died Australia 1955
Australia from 1889; France 1900–13, 1926–31
The yellow screen (**Family group**) 1910–11
painted in Pacé, Brittany, France
oil on canvas mounted on composition board, 217.5 x 140 cm
National Gallery of Australia, Canberra, purchased 1969

The yellow screen is one of Max Meldrum's more intimate paintings; a rarity in an oeuvre predominantly concerned with investigating the optical truths of nature, and in which psychological, personal or literary meanings are given least attention.

Meldrum painted himself alongside his French-born wife and daughter. The young, blonde Ida is posed in a similar manner to Velázquez's depiction of the Infanta Margarita in *Las meninas (The family of Philip V)* c. 1656 (Museo Nacional del Prado, Spain). In this atmospheric, darkened room, Meldrum refers to Velázquez's spatially ambiguous perspective and masterly control of tonal values. In place of Velázquez's canvas, Meldrum depicts a Japanese screen, tonally balancing the composition and perhaps making reference to the popularly embraced aesthetic of Japonisme.

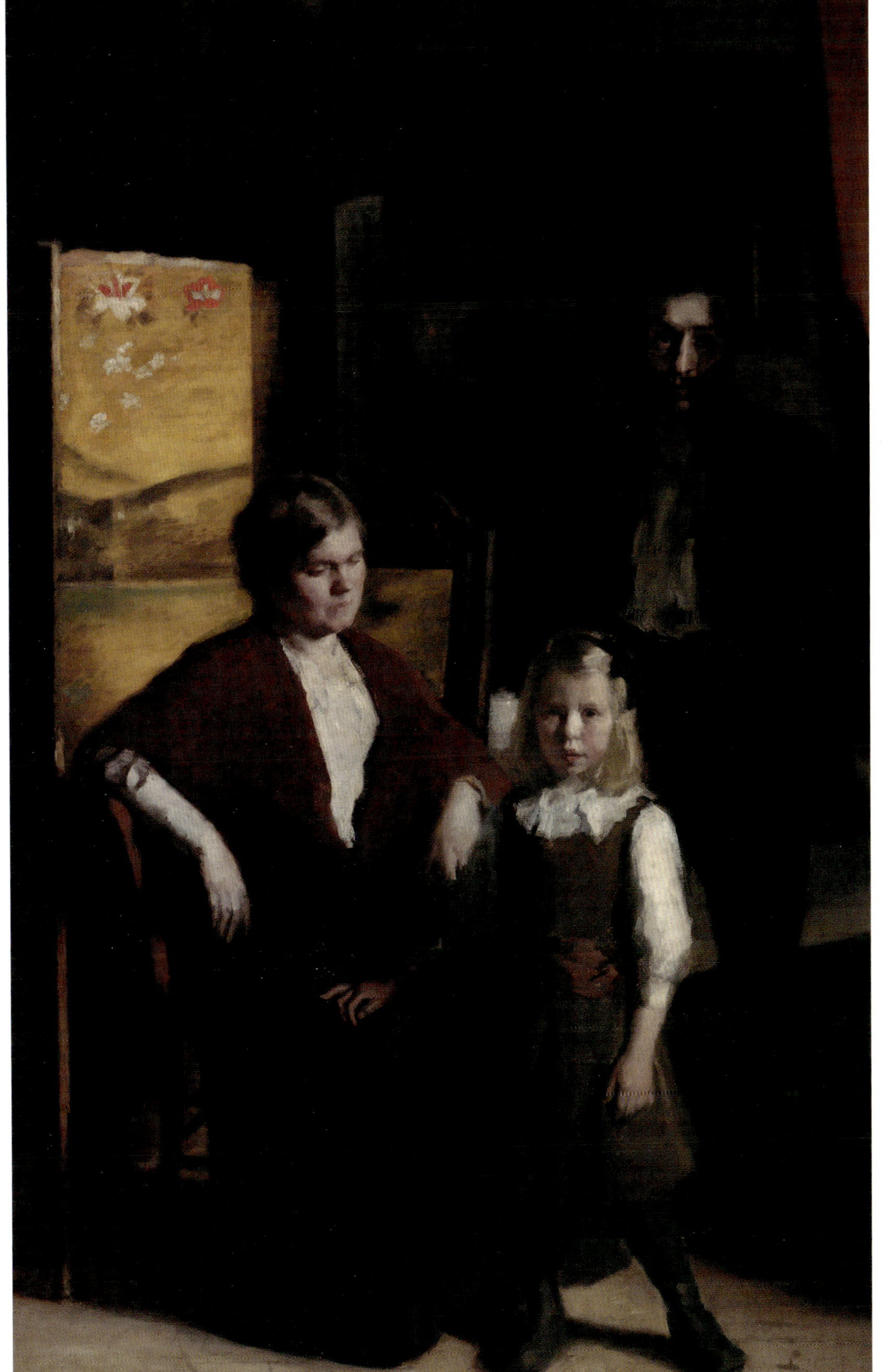

born Scotland 1875 died Australia 1955
Australia from 1889; France 1900–13, 1926–31
Four o'clock c. 1910
painted in Pacé, Brittany, France
oil on canvas, 70.2 x 96.3 cm
National Gallery of Australia, Canberra, purchased 1970

After making connections with a French painter from Rennes, in Brittany,
Max Meldrum spent increasing periods in this region, painting out of doors.
The striking winter sunset captured in Meldrum's *Four o'clock* reveals the influence
of his time spent studying the work of Barbizon School painter Camille Corot in
the grand Musée du Louvre, Paris.

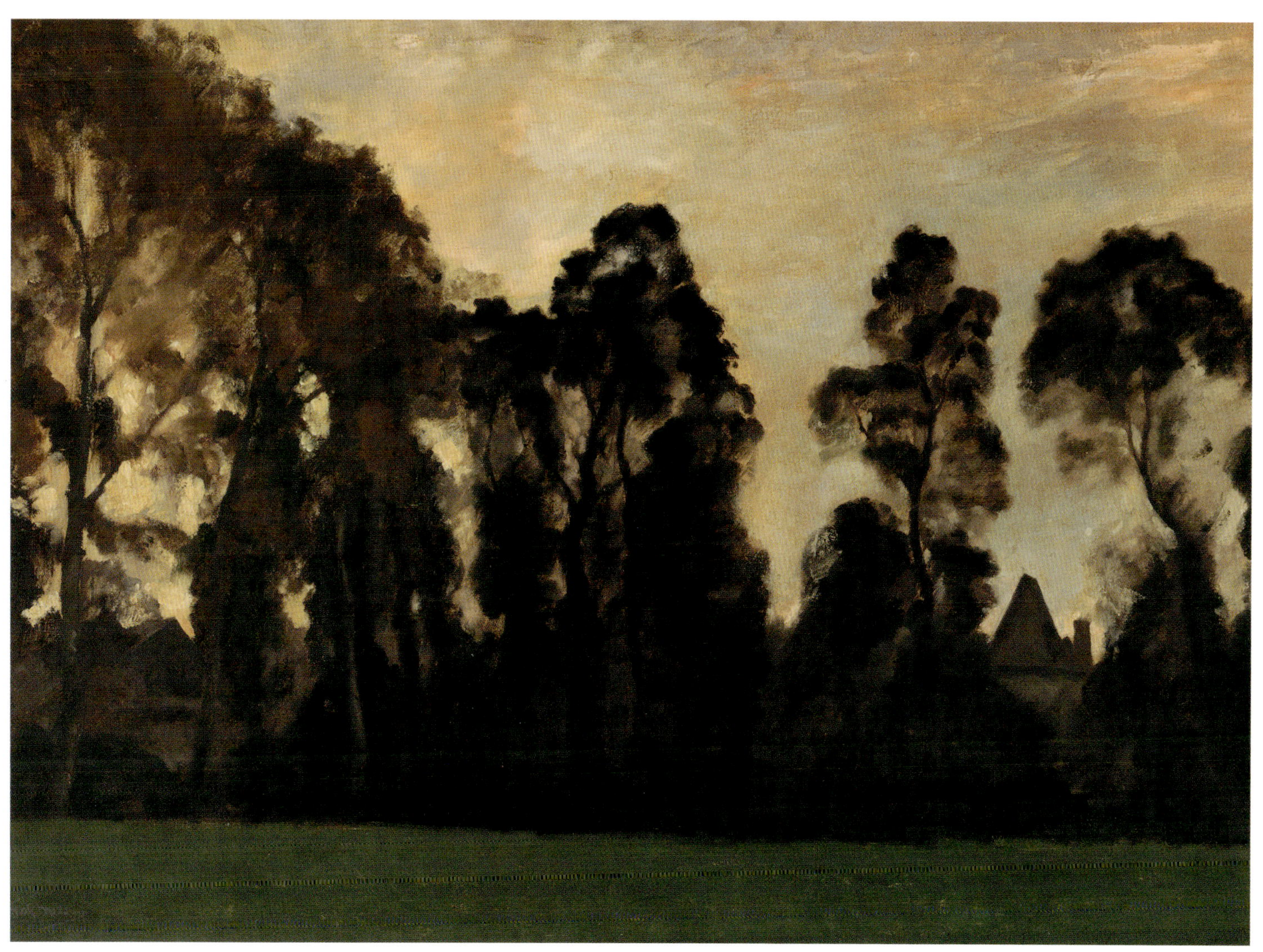

MAX MELDRUM

born Scotland 1875 died Australia 1955
Australia from 1889; France 1900–13, 1926–31
La Flume c. 1910
painted in Pacé, Brittany, France
oil on canvas, 72 x 87.3 cm
National Gallery of Australia, Canberra, purchased 1974

Max Meldrum wrote extensively on art throughout his career. In his essay 'Doctrinaire in art' published in *Triad* (vol. 10, no. 6, 1 April 1925), he reflected on the significance of seeing the works of European Old Masters during his time in France as a student, between 1900 and 1913:

> I wanted to know the meaning of depictive art, and I went to study the art of the past, in order to find out its tradition and progress. I discovered that the whole tradition of depictive art was based on an ever-increasing knowledge of what we see. The study of the Old Masters gave me courage to go and look at nature and study it first hand.

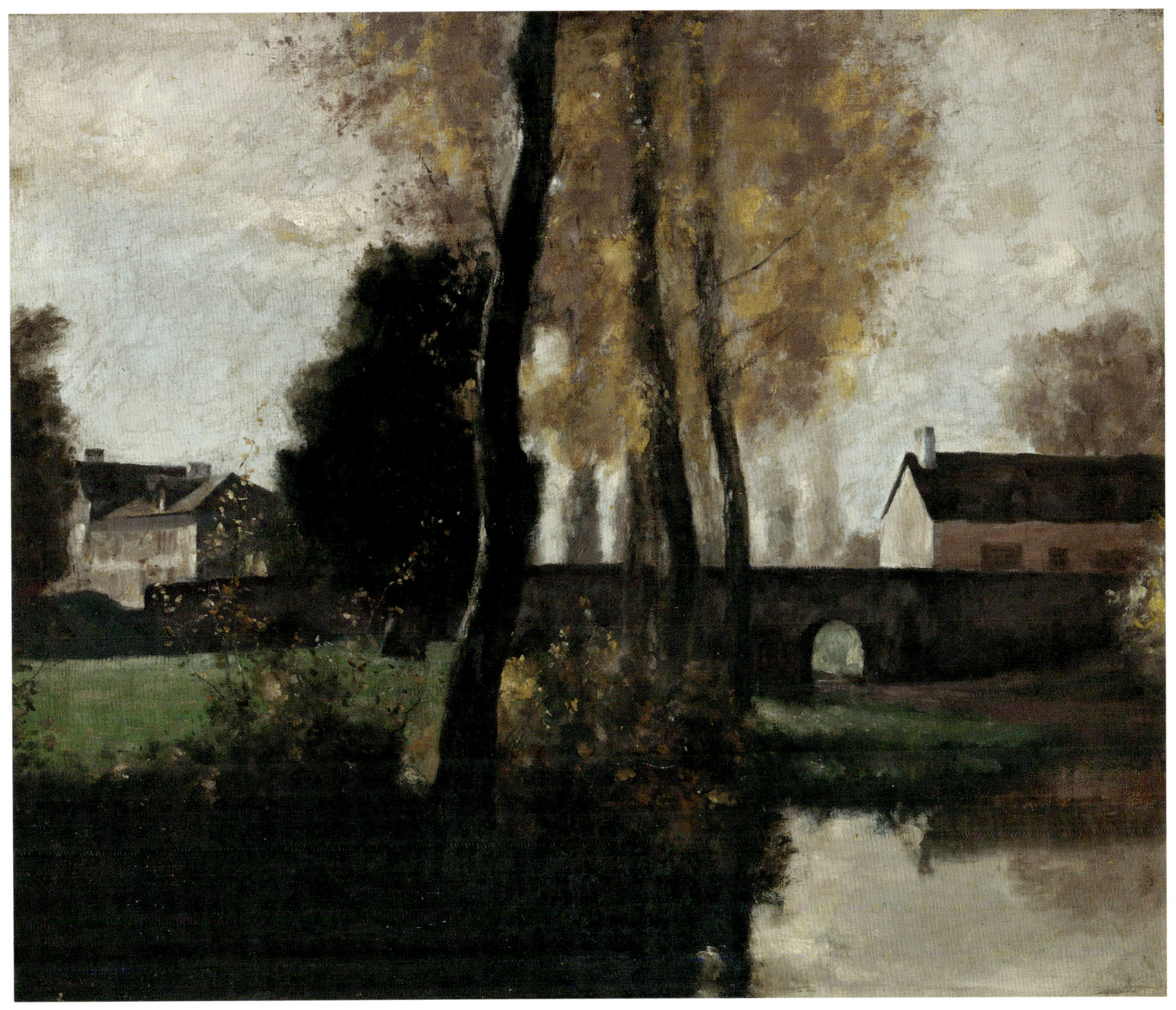

GEORGE BELL

born Australia 1878 died Australia 1966
France, England 1903–19
The beach, *Les Petites-Dalles* 1913
painted in Les Petites-Dalles, Upper Normandy, France
oil on panel, 26.8 x 35 cm
National Gallery of Australia, Canberra, purchased 2007

George Bell left for Europe in 1903, studying first in Paris and later in London, where he settled in 1908. Like most expatriate artists, Bell travelled widely in Europe, painting in locations such as the artists' colonies of Etaples in northern France and St Ives in Cornwall, England, as well as the popular summer holiday destinations, such as Les Petites-Dalles, in the French region of Normandy. The striking cliffs that frame the pebbly beach of Les Petites-Dalles inspired numerous artists, including Claude Monet in the 1880s. Although only housing one guesthouse and one restaurant, the beach attracted holiday crowds over the summer, as depicted in this painting.

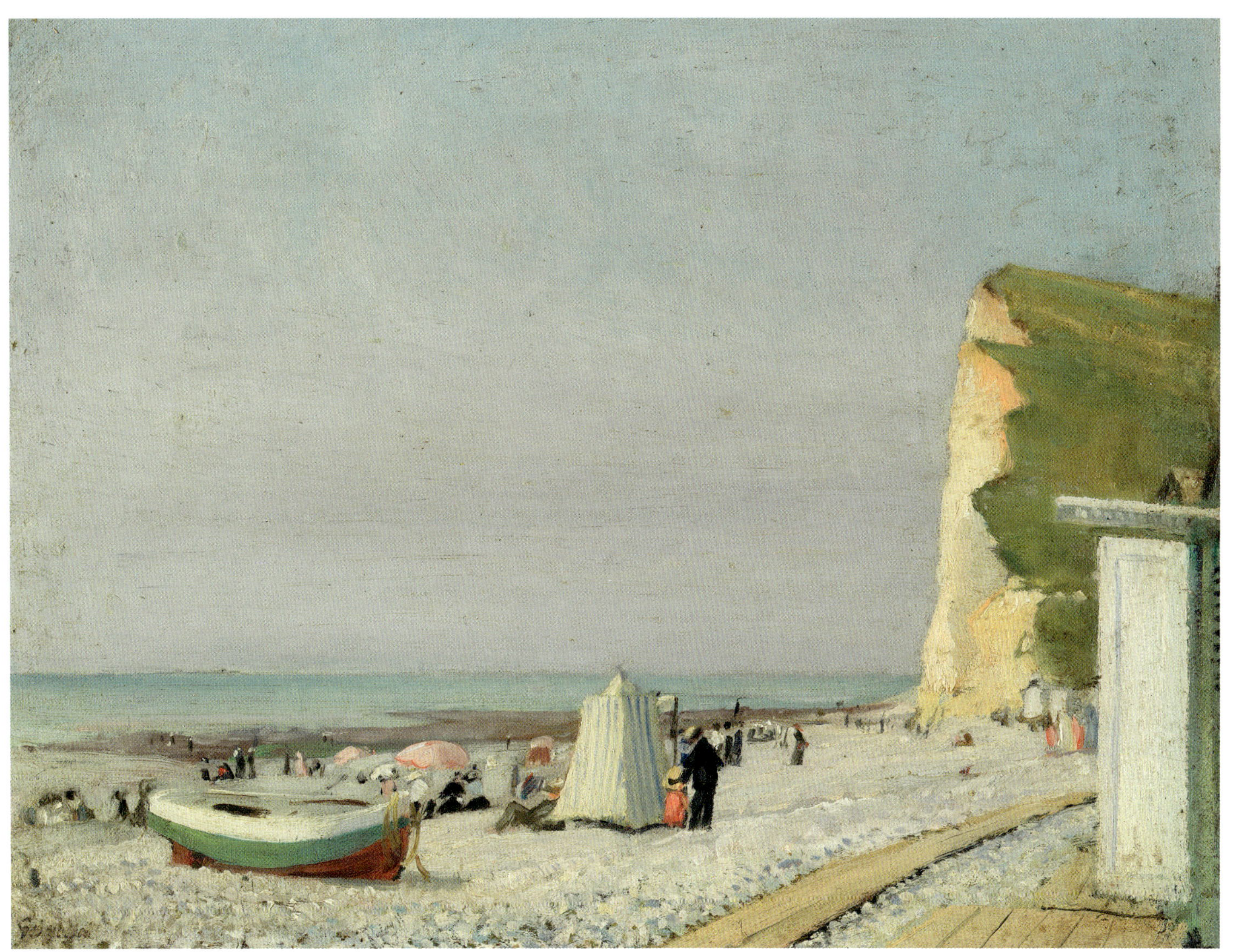

born England 1872 died Australia 1952
France from 1905; Australia 1908, 1913–16, with frequent visits thereafter
At sunset c. 1914
likely to have been painted between Australia and Tahiti
oil on canvas mounted on cardboard, 25 x 31 cm
National Gallery of Australia, Canberra, purchased 1977

Ethel Carrick and E. Phillips Fox had embarked on a painting trip through the Pacific when the First World War broke out in 1914. Returning to Australia, they postponed their return to Paris. Just one year later, Fox died in Melbourne, prompting Carrick to return to Europe in 1916.[21]

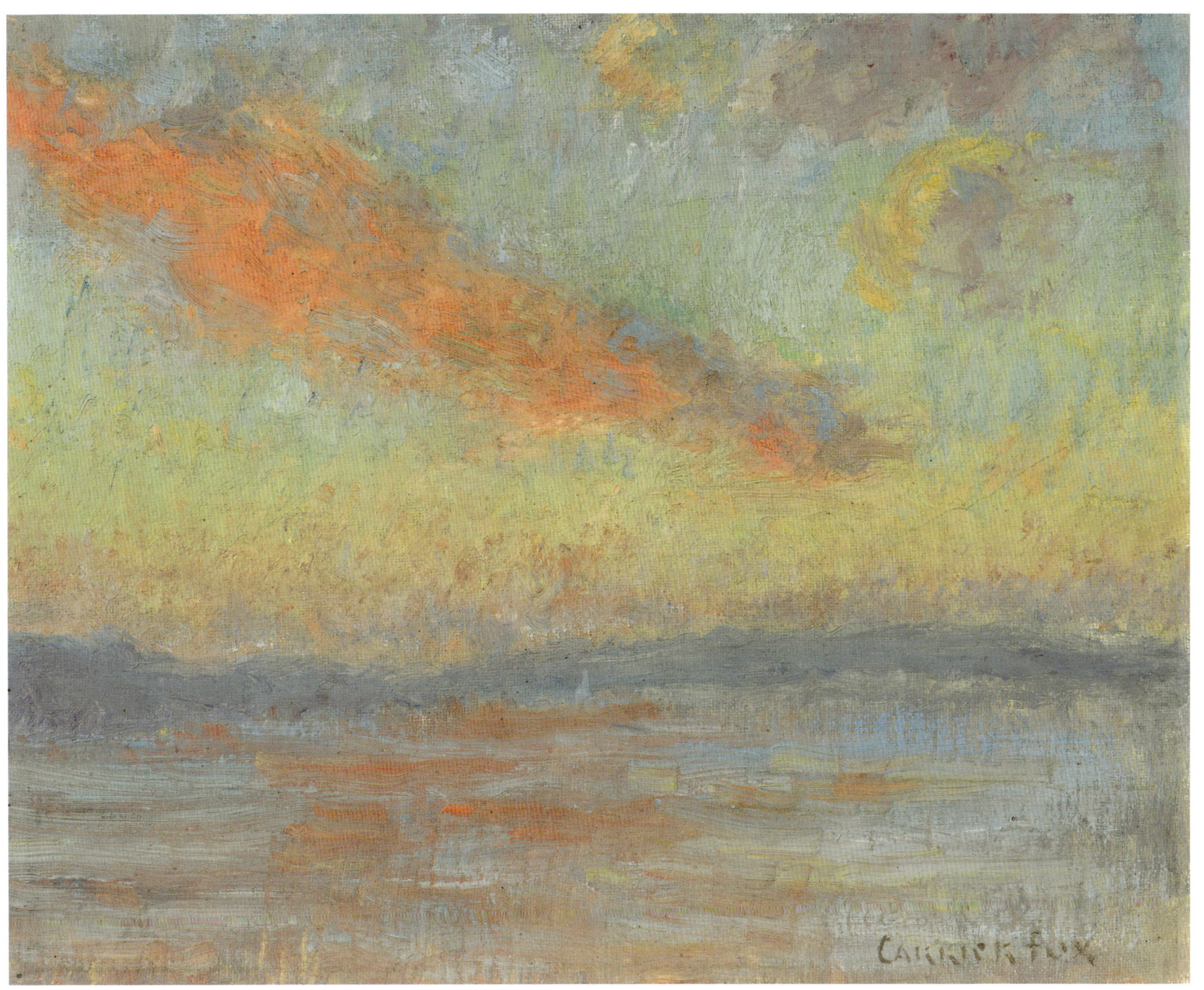

RUPERT BUNNY

born Australia 1864 died Australia 1947
England, France 1884–1933
Shearing: Australia House sketches c. 1914
painted in La Rochefoucauld, France
oil on cardboard, 34 x 45.2 cm (composition)
National Gallery of Australia, Canberra, acquired 1969

*Preparations for the decoration and furnishing of Australia's new house in London
are already considerably advanced. Australian artists are invited by the Minister for
External Affairs (Mr. Glynn), to submit sketches for mural decorations. The terms of
competition to select artists to paint the mural decorations are that it will be open to all
artists born in Australia and who have lived in Australia for five years and upwards, and
who are now resident in Australia. Twelve paintings in all are required, and they are to
depict incidents in Australian history and features of Australian scenery, and of Australian
productive activity. All the sketches, which must be in oil and tempera on canvas, must be
forwarded to the High Commissioner's office, London, not later than January 15, 1915.*
(*Register*, 20 July 1914, and *Argus*, 20 July 1914)

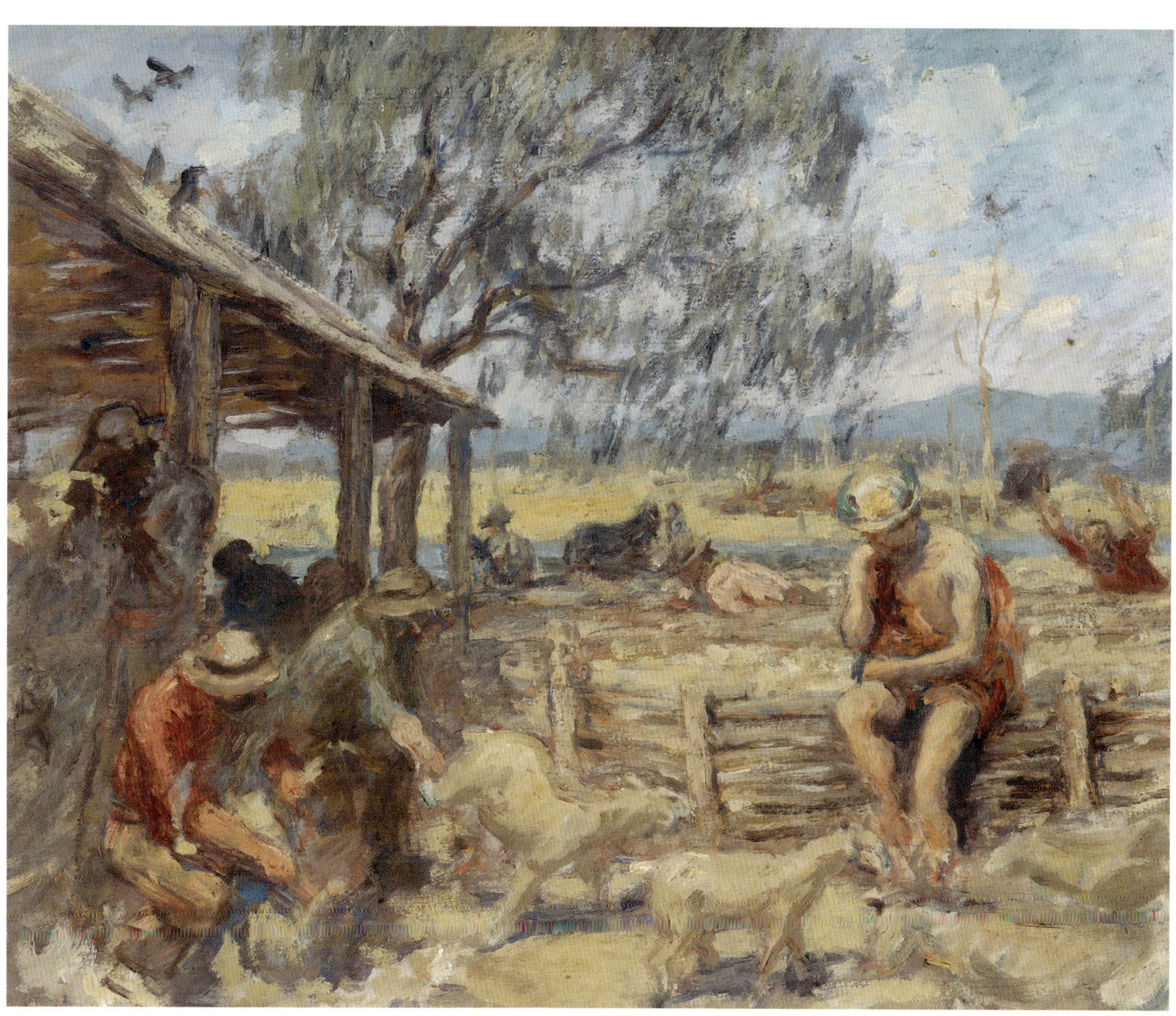

born Australia 1864 died Australia 1947
England, France 1884–1933
Image symbolising the Australian Commonwealth c. 1914
painted in La Rochefoucauld, France
oil on cardboard, 38 x 51 cm
National Gallery of Australia, Canberra, acquired 1969

The development of Australia's diplomatic mission in central London represented
a continuation of British–Australian ties, yet was also symbolic as Australia's first
international diplomatic presence. The embassy became known as 'Australia House'
and was the first official building designed to represent Australia after Federation.
Although the search for an appropriate site had begun soon after Federation,
the site in the Strand was not confirmed until 1911 and building did not start until
1913. In 1914, a competition was advertised in Britain and Australia for Australian
artists to submit designs for a series of murals for major rooms in the building.
The competition, however, was postponed within months with the outbreak of
the First World War.

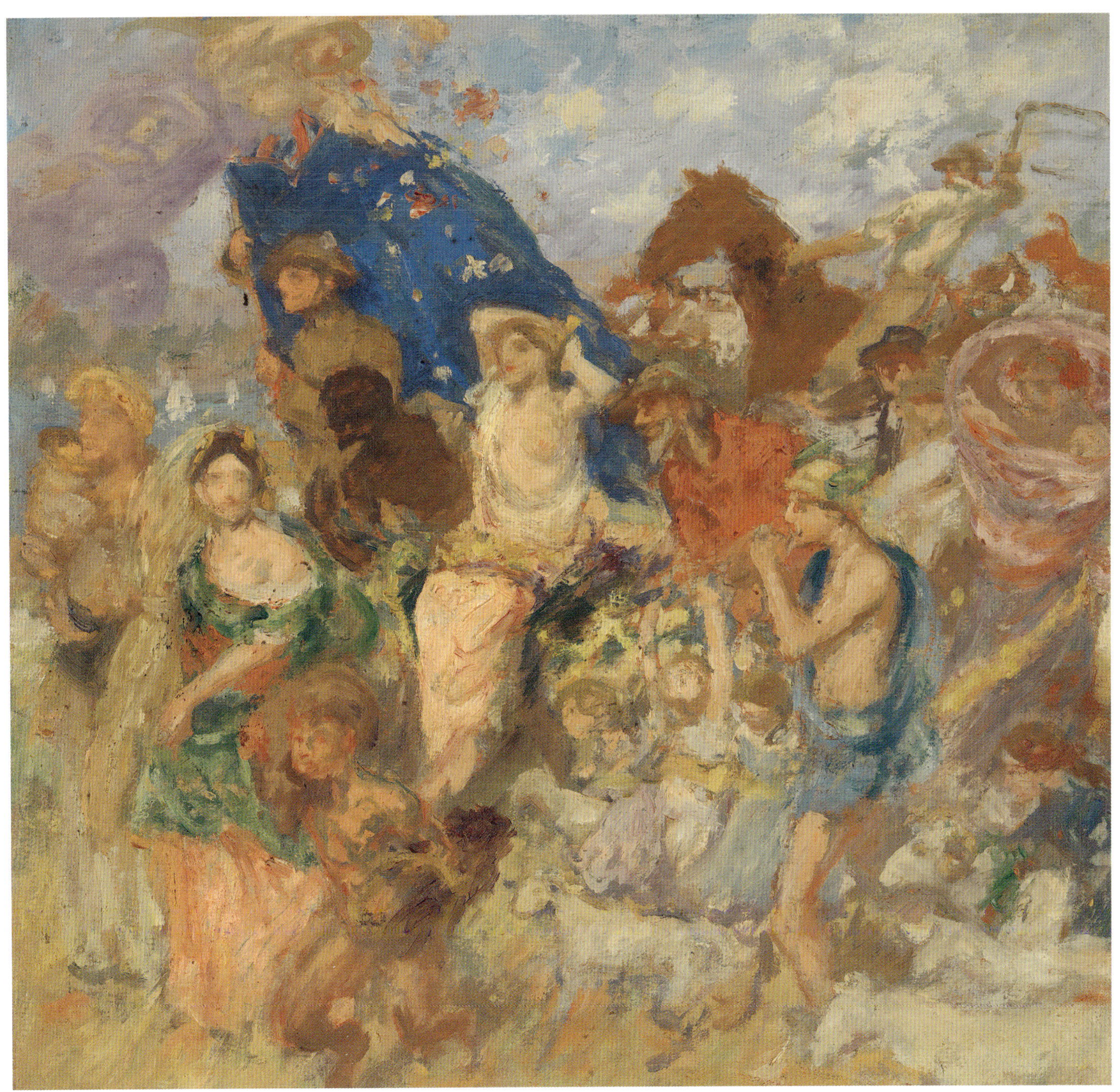

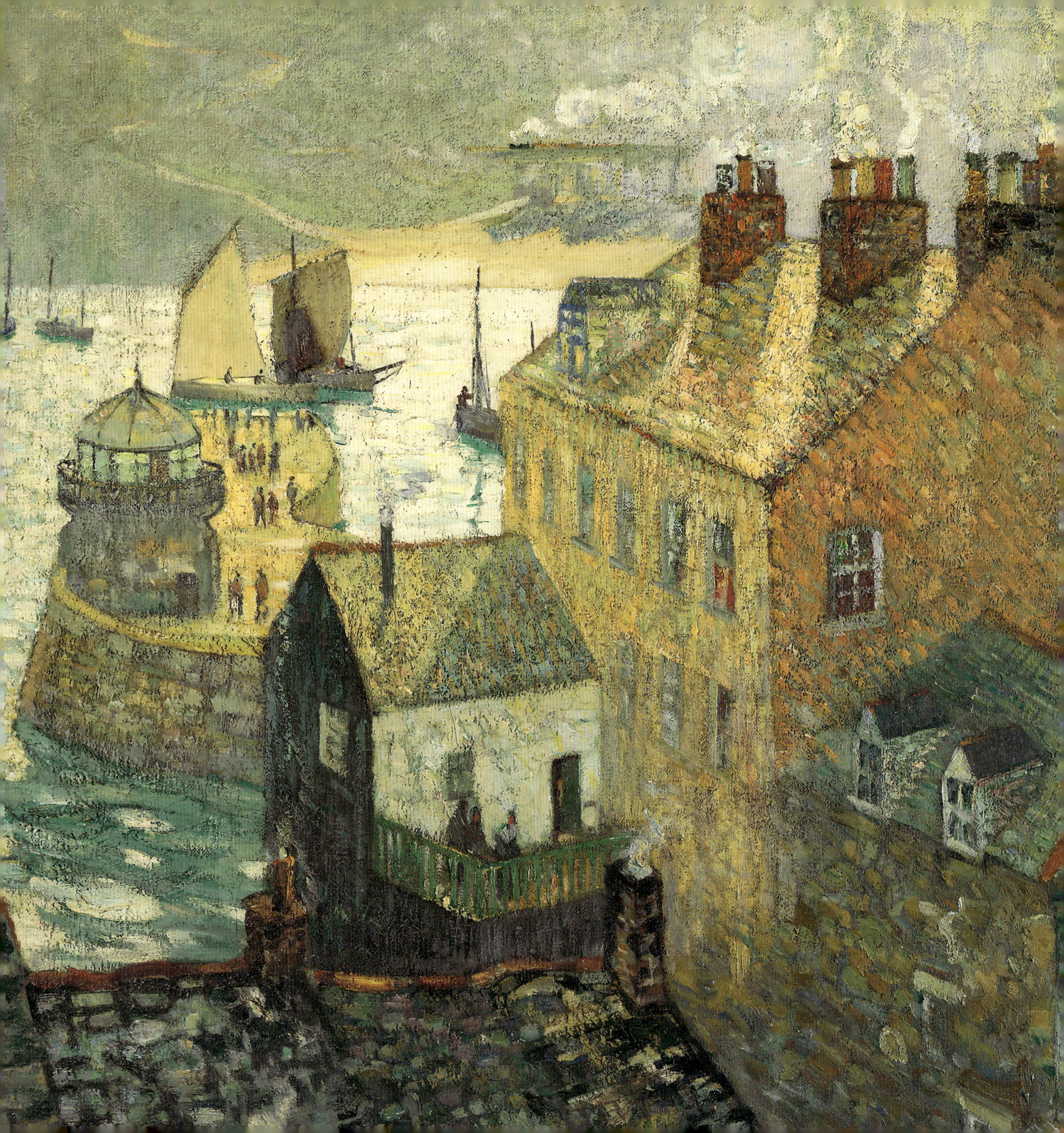

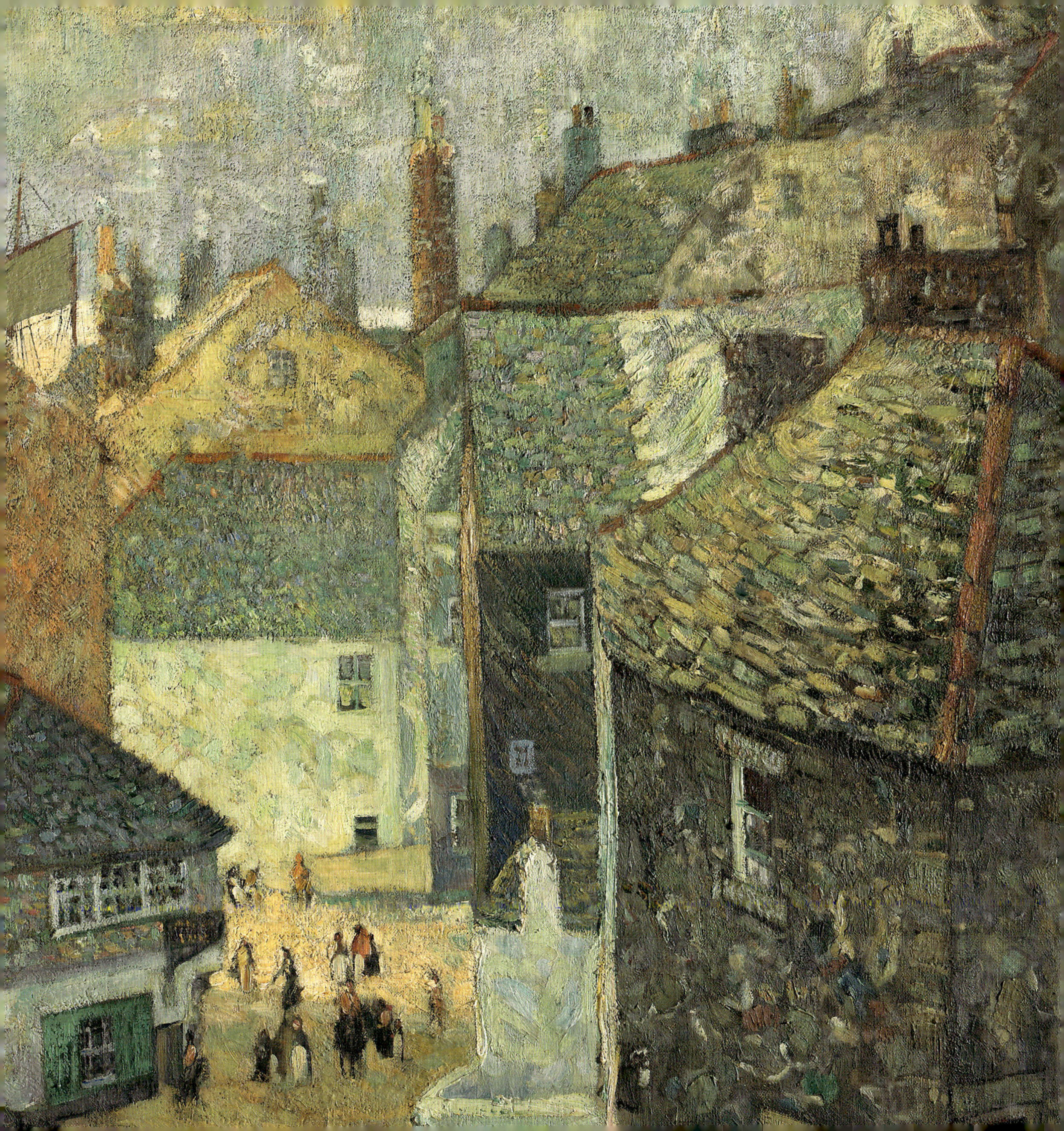

TIMELINE

The events listed are intended as a rough guide to the era, and inevitably there are many events that are not included.

1897

The Art Gallery of South Australia receives a bequest from Sir Thomas Elder, the first significant bequest to a major public art gallery in Australia.

Artists' movements

Arthur Streeton leaves for London/Egypt.

1898

The first annual Federal Exhibition is held in Adelaide, arranged by the South Australian Society of Artists, continuing until 1928.

Artists' movements

W.C. Piguenit visits Britain.

1899

Artists' movements

Hans Heysen leaves for Paris.
Richard Hayley-Lever leaves Paris for St Ives, Cornwall.

1900

17 September, Queen Victoria proclaims that the Commonwealth of Australia, a federation comprising all six colonies, will come into existence on 1 January 1901.

21 September, Queen Victoria officially appoints John Adrian Louis-Hope, Seventh Earl of Hopetoun, as Australia's first Governor-General.

Artists' movements

Hugh Ramsay and Max Meldrum leave for Scotland/Paris.
George W. Lambert leaves for London/Paris.
W.C. Piguenit visits Britain a second time.

1901

1 January, the six colonies of Australia become a federation, known as the Commonwealth of Australia. Melbourne is the temporary capital of Australia until 1927.

Edmund Barton serves as Prime Minister until 1903.

22 January, Queen Victoria dies and Edward VII becomes king.

The Art Society of New South Wales stages *The Federal Art Exhibition* in Sydney.

29 March, the first Australian Federal elections are held.

Edmund Barton selects the first Federal Cabinet.

Discussions regarding the site for the Federal Capital Territory begin.

The Australian population is counted as over 3.8 million in the first Federal census. Aboriginal Australians were not counted as part of this census, but are estimated to have been a population of over 94,000.

The *Immigration Restriction Act* is passed (known as the 'White Australia policy').

9 May, the first Federal Parliament of Australia is declared open by the Duke of Cornwall and York (later King George V) at the Exhibition Building in Melbourne. A week-long celebration is held in Melbourne surrounding the event.

In September the Australian flag is selected from hundreds of designs submitted by the public, and flown for the first time in Melbourne.

Advance Australia Fair written by (P.D. McCormick) is sung at the inauguration ceremony. This song officially becomes Australia's national anthem on 19 April 1984.

The National Council of Women is formed in Victoria.

Artists' movements

E. Phillips Fox leaves for England.

1902

31 May, the Boer War ends in South Africa. Military forces from the Australian colonies that assisted the British from 1899 to 1902 eventually form the basis of Australia's army.

12 June, the *Commonwealth Franchise Act* is formalised, giving all Australian women the right to vote in federal elections.

The Capital Sites Enquiry Board begins investigations for suitable sites within a range of suggested areas. Members of Federal Parliament tour possible sites during 1902 and 1903.

1903

9 January, Lord Tennyson, acting Governor-General from 17 July 1902, is confirmed as the new Governor-General of Australia.

The Commonwealth Parliament inaugurates the High Court of Australia.

24 September, Edmund Barton resigns as Prime Minister to become a judge in the High Court of Australia.

Alfred Deakin serves as Prime Minister until 1904.

Artists' movements

Tom Roberts leaves for Britain to finalise some of the individual portraits for the commissioned painting *Opening of the First Parliament of the Commonwealth of Australia by H.R.H The Duke of Cornwall and York (later King George V), May 9, 1901*. He completes the work in London, and presents it to King Edward VII.

George Bell leaves for France.

Hans Heysen returns to Adelaide.

Hugh Ramsay returns to Melbourne.

1904

21 January, Lord Northcote becomes Governor-General of Australia, serving until 9 September 1908.

Chris Watson serves as Prime Minister during 1904.

George Reid serves as Prime Minister from 1904 until 1905.

The National Gallery of Victoria receives the bequest of Alfred Felton, replacing the Elder bequest as the largest bequest received by a public gallery.

Dorothea Mackellar writes the poem *My country*, first published in 1908 with the title *Core of my heart* in the *Spectator* in London.

Artists' movements

Florence Fuller returns to Australia, living and working in Perth between 1904 and 1908.

1905

Alfred Deakin serves as Prime Minister until 1908.

Artists' movements

E. Phillips Fox and Ethel Carrick marry in London.

1906

5 March, Hugh Ramsay, Australian painter, dies of tuberculosis in Melbourne.

Artists' movements

Arthur Streeton visits Australia, exhibiting in Melbourne and Sydney, returning to London in early 1907.

1907

Artists' movements

Frederick McCubbin visits Britain and France for three months, his first and only trip to Europe.

Hilda Rix Nicholas leaves for London.

1908

9 September, Lord Dudley becomes Australia's fourth Governor-General, serving until 31 July 1911.

8 October, the final vote in the House of Representatives is held for the selection of the region for the Federal Capital. The 'Yass–Canberra' region receives the majority of votes.

Andrew Fisher serves as Prime Minister until 1909.

Artists' movements

E. Phillips Fox and Ethel Carrick visit Australia.

1909

25 February, Surveyor Charles Scrivener and his team complete the final survey of Canberra, building on the earlier work of a small number of engineers and surveyors in the New South Wales Department of Public Works.

Alfred Deakin serves as Prime Minister until 1910.

13 December, the Act establishing an Australian High Commission in London becomes law and Australia's first overseas office is established. George Reid becomes Australia's first High Commissioner.

1910

6 May

Edward VII dies, and George V becomes king.

Andrew Fisher serves as Prime Minister until 1913.

Artists' movements

Sydney Long leaves for London, where he lives and works until returning to Australia permanently in 1925.

1911

1 January, the Northern Territory and the Australian Capital Territory formally come into being and are transferred to the Commonwealth of Australia. The Federal Capital Territory includes an area of 2360 square kilometres and a seaport at Jervis Bay, New South Wales.

30 January, the International Design Competition for Australia's Federal Capital is launched, attracting 137 national and international submissions.

31 July, Lord Denman becomes Governor-General, serving until 18 May 1914.

12 December, the Australian Senate decides on the site for Australia House in London, and the corner site on the Aldwych curve of the Strand is acquired.

A national art collection is founded with a view to collecting for a future Federal gallery.

The Commonwealth Government Historic Memorials Committee is established.

Artists' movements

Richard Hayley-Lever leaves Britain for the United States of America, settling there permanently in 1912.

Penleigh Boyd leaves for Britain.

1912

23 May, Minister for Home Affairs, King O'Malley, announced Walter Burley Griffin and Marion Mahony Griffin as the winners of the International Design Competition for Australia's Federal Capital.

The wattle is declared Australia's national flower and entwined within the Australian Coat of Arms. On 19 September the newly designed Australian Coat of Arms is granted Royal Warrant by King George V.

Artists' movements

Penleigh Boyd returns to Melbourne.

1913

2 January, the first Australian stamp is issued – the Commonwealth penny stamp. It features a kangaroo on a white map of Australia.

20 February, Minister for Home Affairs, King O'Malley, hammers in the first peg to begin the city of Canberra survey on Capital Hill.

12 March, foundation stones for the Federal Capital are laid by the Governor-General, Lord Denman, the Prime Minister, Andrew Fisher and by the Minister for Home Affairs, King O'Malley. Lady Denman announces 'Canberra' as the name of the Federal Capital.

Joseph Cook serves as Prime Minister until 1914.

July, the foundation stone of Australia House is laid on the site in The Strand, London. Construction was completed in 1918, delayed by the First World War.

August 18, Walter Burley Griffin arrives in Australia to visit the Canberra site.

The National Gallery of Victoria, Melbourne, acquires two important European Impressionist works with the Felton bequest: Claude Monet's *Gros Temps à Etretat* [*Rough weather at Etretat*] 1883; and Alfred Sisley's *Les Meules de paille à Moret – effet du matin* [*Haystacks at Moret – morning light*] 1891.

W. Lister Lister is announced as the winner of the competition to paint the site of the Federal Capital. Penleigh Boyd is awarded an unplanned-for second prize. Both works are acquired by the Federal Government's Historic Memorials Committee.

Artists movements

E. Phillips Fox and Ethel Carrick return to Melbourne.

Max Meldrum returns to Melbourne.

1914

Andrew Fisher serves as Prime Minister until 1915.

A competition to design murals for the interior of Australia House in London is launched for Australian artists working in London and Australia. The competition is cancelled shortly afterwards with the outbreak of the First World War.

4 August, the First World War begins.

Capital and country: the Federation years 1900–1913

1 The term 'country' in the title of this exhibition implies impressions of countryside or landscape in the European tradition, rather than the land itself as the source of Aboriginal Australian culture in the Indigenous tradition.

2 Alfred Deakin, *Morning Post*, London, 8 January 1901, cited in Raymond Evans et al, *1901: our future's past*, Macmillan, Sydney, 1997, p. 170.

3 Quoted in R.H. Croll, *Tom Roberts: father of Australian landscape painting*, Robertson & Mullens, Melbourne, 1935, p. 62. See also Ron Radford, *Our country: Australian Federation landscapes 1900–1914*, Art Gallery of South Australia, Adelaide, 2001, pp. 25–6.

4 As above.

5 R.M. Crawford, 'Tom Roberts and Alfred Deakin', in Franz Philipp & June Steward (eds), *In honour of Daryl Lindsay*, Oxford University Press, Melbourne, 1964, p. 163.

6 See Leigh Astbury, *Sunlight and shadow: Australian Impressionist painters 1880–1900*, Bay Books, Sydney, 1989, p. 206.

7 For further discussion, see, for example, Richard White, *Inventing Australia: images and identity 1788–1980*, Allen & Unwin, Sydney, 1981, p.111.

8 Lionel Wigmore, *Canberra*, 2nd edn, Dalton Publishing, Canberra, 1971, p. 26.

9 Wigmore, 1971, pp. 26, 33.

10 A. Fisher, 'Notice to landscape artists', *Commonwealth of Australia Gazette*, no. 80, 21 December 1912, p. 2639, cited in Radford, 2001, pp. 123–4.

11 Croll, 1935, p. 62.

12 White, 1981, p. 87.

13 J.F. Paterson, 'Australian art: lack of originality', in *Argus*, Melbourne, 20 July 1906, p. 7.

14 Radford, 2001, p. 120.

15 For further discussion, see, for example, Ian Burn et al, *The necessity of Australian art: an essay about interpretation*, University of Sydney Printing Services, Sydney, 1988, p. 15; and Radford, 2001, p. 132.

16 'Hans Heysen's brush: a visit to the studio', *Advertiser*, Adelaide, 18 May 1904, p. 6.

17 Radford, 2001, p. 50.

18 Hans Heysen to Lionel Lindsay 20 March 1912, cited in Colin Thiele, *Heysen of Hahndorf*, Rigby, Adelaide, 1969, p. 288.

19 Heysen in notes from interviews with Ian Mudie and Colin Thiele 1966–67, quoted in Thiele, p. 311.

20 Radford, 2001, p. 60.

21 The 'bush' at this time refers to unpopulated areas of native forest, as well as the semi-rural regions of lightly settled, cleared pastoral land, and was romanticised in art, literature and poetry.

22 *The studio*, London, September 1909, p. 69, quoted in Jane Clark, 'The scent of eucalypts', in Daniel Thomas & Ron Radford (eds), *Creating Australia: 200 years of art 1788–1988*, International Cultural Association with Art Gallery of South Australia Board, Adelaide, 1988, p. 100.

23 Anne Gray, *McCubbin: last impressions 1907–17*, National Gallery of Australia, Canberra, 2009, p. 32.

24 McCubbin to Roberts, 27 January 1909, Letters to Tom Roberts, MS A2478, vol. 2, no. 18, Mitchell Library, State Library of New South Wales, Sydney, cited in Gray, 2009, p. 90.

25 Frederick McCubbin, 'Some remarks about Australian art', in J.S. MacDonald, *The art of Frederick McCubbin*, Lothian Book Publishing Co., Melbourne, 1916, p. 84.

26 *Argus*, 1 May 1913, p. 5; and explored further in Mary Eagle, 'Flood Waters 1913', in Gray, 2009, p. 132.

27 McCubbin in MacDonald, 1916, pp. 91, 94.

28 Rivers, 'Sunlight in Pictures', *Queensland Art Society Annual Report*, 1898, p. 25, cited in Lynne Sear & Julie Ewington (eds.), *Brought to light: Australian art 1850–1965*, Queensland Art Gallery, Brisbane, 1998, p. 91.

29 Sydney Long, 'The trend in Australian art considered and discussed', *Art and Architecture*, Sydney, vol. II, 1905, pp. 8–10.

30 As above.

31 Beatrice Gralton, 'Harry Garlick, *The drover* 1906', in Ron Radford, *Ocean to outback: Australian landscape painting 1850–1950*, National Gallery of Australia, Canberra, 2007, p. 75.

32 Caroline Ford, 'Lifesaver', in Melissa Harper & Richard White (eds), *Symbols of Australia: uncovering the stories behind the myths*, University of New South Wales Press, Sydney, National Museum of Australia, Canberra, 2010, p. 154.

33 It was not until the late twentieth century that Federation landscape painting began to be reassessed. Since the turn of twenty-first century, within the context of celebrations of the centenary of Federation, the era's major painters and their key contributions to the story of Australian painting have also been more closely examined. See Radford, 2001.

34 Kate Henderson has noted in her 2008 entry on Ramsay in the Dictionary of Australian Artists Online that he was supported by the proceeds of an 'art union', a type of lottery of works for paying subscribers. (daao.org.au/bio/version_history/hugh-ramsay/biography/?revision_no=27).

35 Hugh Ramsay to Baldwin Spencer, 12 February 1901, Baldwin Spencer papers, Mitchell Library, Sydney, cited in Patricia Fullerton, *Hugh Ramsay: his life and work*, Hudson Publishing, Melbourne, 1988, p. 55.

36 Hugh Ramsay to his sisters, Nellie, Maggie and Jessie Ramsay, 28 March 1901, Ramsay letter archive, National Gallery of Australia, Canberra, IRN5830, pp. 2–3.

37 Hugh Ramsay to Bernard Hall, 19 June 1902, Bernard Hall archive, National Gallery of Australia Research Library, Canberra, 2BH434.

38 Max Meldrum, 'Doctrinaire in art', *Triad*, vol. 10, no. 6, 1 April 1925, p. 10.

39 Anne Gray, 'The Edwardians', in *The Edwardians: secrets and desires*, National Gallery of Australia, Canberra, 2004, p. 20.

40 Lambert in his unpublished 'Autobiography of George Lambert', [1924], Lambert Family Papers, Mitchell Library, Sydney, ML MSS A1811, cited in Anne Gray, *George W. Lambert retrospective: heroes and icons*, National Gallery of Australia, Canberra, 2007, p. 102.

41 Mary Eagle, *The oil paintings of E. Phillips Fox in the National Gallery of Australia*, National Gallery of Australia, Canberra, 1997, pp. 35–36.

42 Gray, 2004, pp. 39, 99.

43 Ruth Zubans, *E. Phillips Fox: his life and art*, Melbourne University Press, 1995, p. 93.

44 Zubans, 1995, p. 137.

45 Mary Eagle, *The art of Rupert Bunny in the Australian National Gallery*, Australian National Gallery, Canberra, 1991, p. 60.

46 Works such as *Qui vient?* [*Who comes?*] c. 1908, were first shown in London under the title, 'Days and nights in August'. See Eagle, 1991, pp. 60, 68.

47 Arthur Streeton to Tom Roberts, 28 June 1898, in Anne Gray & Ann Galbally (eds), *Letters from Smike: the letters of Arthur Streeton* 1890–1943, Oxford University Press, Melbourne, 1989, p. 78.

48 'Our artists abroad: a chat with Arthur Streeton', *Sydney Morning Herald*, 31 December 1906, p. 7.

49 Croll, 1935, p. 38.

50 Hugh Ramsay to Harry Ramsay, 1 August 1901, Ramsay letter archive, National Gallery of Australia, Canberra, IRN5835, p. 7.

The paintings

1 Hans Heysen, cited in William Moore, *The story of Australian art: from the earliest known art of the continent to the art of to-day*, 1934, p. 87.

2 From *The closed door and other verses*, Australasian Authors' Agency, Melbourne, 1911.

3 Rivers, 'Sunlight in pictures', *Queensland Art Society Annual Report*, 1898, p. 25, cited in Lynne Sear & Julie Ewington (eds), *Brought to light: Australian art 1850–1965*, Queensland Art Gallery, Brisbane, 1998, p. 91.

4 Katie Holmes, *Between the leaves: stories of Australian women, writing and gardens*, University of Western Australia, Perth, 2011, pp. 19–35.

5 As above.

6 Anne Gray, *McCubbin: last impressions 1907–1917*, National Gallery of Australia, Canberra, 2009, p. 57.

7 As above.

8 Tom Roberts letters, ML: Letters to Tom Roberts, MS A2478, vol. 2, no. 18, Mitchell Library, State Library of New South Wales, cited in Gray, 2009, p. 90.

9 Jane Clark, 'Introduction', *Violet Teague*, The Beagle Press, Sydney, 1999, p. 9.

10 Barry Pearce, *Elioth Gruner, 1882–1939*, Art Gallery of New South Wales, Sydney, 1983, p. 14.

11 McCubbin, in *The art of Frederick McCubbin*, 1916, p. 84

12 From Geraldine Rede, *A little book of trees*, Melbourne, p. 7, National Gallery of Australia collection, Canberra, NGA 85.1903.9.

13 From the agreement between Hans Heysen and the four Adelaide businessmen, cited in Colin Thiele, *Heysen of Hahndorf*, Rigby, Adelaide, 1968, p. 43.

14 Cited in Mary Eagle, *The oil paintings of Arthur Streeton in the National Gallery of Australia*, National Gallery of Australia, Canberra, 1994, p. 145.

15 Arthur Streeton to Tom Roberts, 14 February 1902, cited in Ann Gallbally & Anne Gray (eds), *Letters from Smike: the letters of Arthur Streeton 1890–1943*, Melbourne: Oxford University Press, 1989, p.90.

16 Arthur Streeton to Baldwin Spencer, 8 October 1908, cited in Gallbally & Gray, 1989, p.114.

17 Eagle, 1994, p. 148.

18 E. Phillips Fox to Norman Carter, 10 September 1909, Norman Carter Papers, State Library of New South Wales, Mitchell Library, ML MS 471/1, cited in Zubans, 1995, p.181.

19 Roberts, cited in Eagle, *The oil paintings of Tom Roberts in the National Gallery of Australia*, National Gallery of Australia, Canberra, 1997, p. 96.

20 Roberts Family papers, cited in Eagle, 1997, p. 97.

21 Angela Goddard, 'An artistic marriage', in *Art, love and life: Ethel Carrick and E. Phillips Fox*, Queensland Art Gallery / Gallery of Modern Art, Brisbane, 2011, pp. 25, 150.

Books

Anderson, Jaynie (ed.), *The Cambridge companion to Australian art*, Cambridge University Press, Melbourne / Cambridge, 2011

Astbury, Leigh, *Sunlight and shadow: Australian Impressionist painters* 1880–1900, Bay Books, Sydney, 1989

Brady, Edwin J., *Australia unlimited*, G. Robertson, Melbourne, 1918

Burn, Ian et al, *The necessity of Australian art: an essay about interpretation*, University of Sydney Printing Services, Sydney, 1988.

Burn, Ian, *National life and landscapes: Australian painting 1900–1940*, Bay Books, Sydney, 1990

Carroll, John (ed.), *Intruders in the bush: the quest for identity*, 2nd edition, Oxford University Press, Melbourne, 1992

Clark, Jane & Druce, Felicity (eds), *Violet Teague*, exhibition catalogue, The Beagle Press, Melbourne, 1999

Cooper-Lavery, Tracey et al, *Wild Colonials: Australian artists & the Newlyn & St Ives colonies*, exhibition catalogue, Bendigo Art Gallery, Bendigo, 2009

Croll, R.H., *Tom Roberts: father of Australian landscape painting*, Robertson & Mullens, Melbourne, 1935

Darian-Smith, Kate et al (eds), *Seize the day: exhibitions, Australia and the world*, Monash University Press, Melbourne, 2008

De Vries, Susanna, *Ethel Carrick Fox: travels and triumphs of a post-Impressionist*, Pandanus, Brisbane, 1997

Edwards, Deborah, with essays by Denise Mimmocchi et al, *Rupert Bunny: artist in Paris*, exhibition catalogue, Art Gallery of New South Wales, Sydney, 2009

Eagle, Mary, *The art of Rupert Bunny in the Australian National Gallery*, Australian National Gallery, Canberra, 1991

Eagle, Mary, *The oil paintings of Arthur Streeton in the National Gallery of Australia*, National Gallery of Australia, Canberra, 1994

Eagle, Mary, *The oil paintings of E. Phillips Fox in the National Gallery of Australia*, National Gallery of Australia, Canberra, 1997

Eagle, Mary, *The oil paintings of Tom Roberts in the National Gallery of Australia*, National Gallery of Australia, Canberra, 1997

Eagle, Mary & Jones, John, *A story of Australian art*, Macmillan, Sydney, 1992

Evans, Raymond et al, *1901: our future's past*, Macmillan, Sydney, 1997

Goddard, Angela et al, *Art, love & life: Ethel Carrick and E. Phillips Fox*, exhibition catalogue, Queensland Art Gallery / Gallery of Modern Art, Brisbane, 2011

Fullerton, Patricia, *Hugh Ramsay: his life and work*, Hudson Publishing, Melbourne, 1988

Galbally, Ann & Gray, Anne (eds), *Letters from Smike: the letters of Arthur Streeton 1890–1943*, Oxford University Press, Melbourne, 1989

Gray, Anne, *Line, light and shadow: James W.R. Linton, painter, craftsman, teacher*, exhibition catalogue, Fremantle Arts Centre Press, Fremantle, 1986

Gray, Anne, *George W. Lambert retrospective: heroes and icons*, exhibition catalogue, National Gallery of Australia, Canberra, 2007

Gray, Anne (ed.), *Australian Art in the National Gallery of Australia*, National Gallery of Australia, Canberra, 2002

Gray, Anne, with essays by Ann Galbally et al, *The Edwardians: secrets and desires*, exhibition catalogue, National Gallery of Australia, Canberra, 2004

Gray, Anne, *McCubbin: last impressions 1907–17*, exhibition catalogue, National Gallery of Australia, Canberra, 2009

Gray, Anne, *Face: Australian portraits 1880–1960*, exhibition catalogue, National Gallery of Australia, Canberra, 2010

Gray, Anne, *Sydney Long: the Spirit of the land*, exhibition catalogue, National Gallery of Australia, Canberra, 2012

Hirst, John, *The sentimental nation: the making of the Australian commonwealth*, Oxford University Press, Melbourne, 2000

Harper, Melissa & White, Richard (eds), *Symbols of Australia*, University of New South Wales Press, Sydney and National Museum of Australia, Canberra, 2010

Holmes, Katie, *Between the leaves: stories of Australian women, writing and gardens*, University of Western Australia Publishing, Perth, 2011

Hoorn, Jeanette (ed.), *Strange women: essays in art and gender*, Melbourne University Press, Melbourne, 1994

Hoorn, Jeanette, *Australian pastoral: the making of a white landscape*, The Fremantle Press, Freemantle, 2007

Hylton, Jane & Neylon, John, *Hans Heysen: into the light*, exhibition catalogue, Wakefield Press, Adelaide, 2004

Johannes, Christa E. & Brown, Anthony V., *W.C. Piguenit 1836–1914 retrospective*, exhibition catalogue, Tasmanian Museum and Art Gallery, Hobart, 1992

Leonard, John, *Australian verse: an Oxford anthology*, Oxford University Press, Melbourne, 1998

Lock-Weir, Tracey, *Misty Moderns: Australian tonalists 1915–1950*, exhibition catalogue, Art Gallery of South Australia, Adelaide, 2008

Lowrey, Carol, *Hayley Lever (1876–1958)*, exhibition catalogue, Spanierman Gallery, New York, 2003

McDonald, John, *Federation: Australian art and society* 1901–2001, exhibition catalogue, National Gallery of Australia, Canberra, 2001

MacDonald, J.S., *The art of Frederick McCubbin*, Lothian Book Publishing Co., Melbourne, 1916

MacDonald, J.S., *The landscapes of Penleigh Boyd*, exhibition catalogue, Alexander McCubbin, Melbourne, 1920

Mackellar, Dorothea, *The closed door and other verses*, Australasian Authors' Agency, Melbourne, 1911

Mimmocchi, Denise, *Australian Symbolism: the art of dreams*, exhibition catalogue, Art Gallery of New South Wales, Sydney, 2012

Moore, William, *The story of Australian art: from the earliest known art of the continent to the art of to-day*, Angus & Robertson, Sydney, 1934

Pearce, Barry, *Elioth Gruner 1882–1939*, exhibition catalogue, Art Gallery of New South Wales, Sydney, 1983

Perry, Peter & John, *Max Meldrum and his associates: their art lives and influences*, exhibition catalogue, Castlemaine Art Gallery and Historical Museum, Castlemaine, 1996

Philipp, Franz & Steward, June (eds), *In honour of Daryl Lindsay*, Oxford University Press, Melbourne, 1964

Radford, Ron et al, *Tom Roberts*, exhibition catalogue, Art Gallery of South Australia, Adelaide, 1996

Radford, Ron, *Our country: Federation landscapes 1900–1914*, exhibition catalogue, Art Gallery of South Australia, Adelaide, 1999

Radford, Ron, *Ocean to outback: Australian landscape painting 1850–1950*, exhibition catalogue, National Gallery of Australia, Canberra, 2007

Radford, Ron (ed.), *Collection highlights: National Gallery of Australia*, National Gallery of Australia, Canberra, 2008

Sayers, Andrew, *Australian art*, Oxford University Press, Oxford, 2001

Sear, Lynne & Ewington, Julie (eds), *Brought to light: Australian art 1850–1965*, Queensland Art Gallery, Brisbane, 1998

Smith, Bernard, *Australian painting 1788–1990*, 3rd edition, with three additional chapters on Australian painting since 1970 by Terry Smith, Oxford University Press, Melbourne, 1991

Smith, Terry, *Transformations in Australian art: the nineteenth century — landscape, colony and nation*, Craftsman House, Sydney, 2002

Thiele, Colin, *Heysen of Hahndorf*, Rigby, Adelaide, 1969

Thomas, Daniel & Radford, Ron (eds), *Creating Australia: 200 years of art 1788–1988*, exhibition catalogue, International Cultural Association with Art Gallery of South Australia Board, Adelaide, 1988

Thomas, David, *Rupert Bunny 1864–1947*, exhibition catalogue, Lansdowne, Melbourne, 1970

Waterhouse, B.J. *Sydney Long A.R.E., loan exhibition*, Art Gallery of New South Wales, Sydney, 1941

White, Richard, *Inventing Australia: images and identity 1688–1980*, Allen & Unwin, Sydney, 1981

Wigmore, Lionel, *Canberra*, revised edition, Dalton Publishing, Canberra, 1971

Wray, Christopher, *Arthur Streeton: painter of light*, Jacaranda Wiley, Milton, 1993

Zubans, Ruth, *Phillips Fox: his life and art*, Melbourne University Press, Melbourne, 1995

Articles

Gray, Anne, 'Hilda Rix Nicholas: Snow Montmartre c. 1914', in *artonview*, issue 56, summer 2008–09, p. 30

Gray, Anne, 'Florence Fuller: Dawn landscape c. 1905', in *artonview*, issue 67, spring 2011, p. 22

Long, Sydney, 'The trend in Australian art considered and discussed', *Art and Architecture*, Sydney, vol. II, 1905, pp. 8–10

Meldrum, Max, 'Doctrinaire in art', *Triad*, vol. 10, no. 6, 1 April 1925, p. 10

Paterson, J.F., 'Australian art: lack of originality', in *Argus*, 20 July 1906, p. 7

Plant, Margaret, 'The lost art of federation: Australia's quest for modernism', in *Art bulletin of Victoria*, National Gallery of Victoria, no. 28, 1987, pp. 111–129

Newspapers

Advertiser, Adelaide, 18 May 1904; 19 December 1912

Age, Melbourne, 10 February 1894; 7 May 1901

Arena, Melbourne, 20 October 1900

Argus, Melbourne, 10 May 1901; 30 May 1911; 21 May 1913; 11 March 1914; 20 July 1914

Brisbane Courier, Brisbane, 25 November 1905

Bulletin, Melbourne, Red Page, 21 May 1908

Daily Telegraph, Sydney, 11 June 1919; 9 June 1927

Register, Adelaide, 7 October 1903; 3 May 1909; 20 July 1914; 14 July 1925

Sydney Morning Herald, Sydney, 7 September 1891; 23 January 1901; 31 December 1906; 22 September 1911; 12 July 1913; 6 August 1913

Table Talk, Melbourne, 25 July 1901

West Australian, Perth, 13 March 1907

Archives

Bernard Hall archive, National Gallery of Australia Research Library, Canberra

Hugh Ramsay letter archive, National Gallery of Australia, Canberra

Online

[http://canberra100.com.au]

Australian Dictionary of Biography, National Centre of Biography, Australian National University, Canberra [http://adb.anu.edu.au]:

Duke, Anne, 'Southern, Clara (1860–1940)'

Galbally, Ann E., 'Streeton, Sir Arthur Ernest (1867–1943)'

Hill, A. J., 'Hutton, Sir Edward Thomas Henry (1848–1923)'

Mitchell, Avenel, 'Nicholas, Emily Hilda (1884–1961)'

Mulvaney, D.J., 'Spencer, Sir Walter Baldwin (1860–1929)'

Pearce, Barry, 'Gruner, Elioth Lauritz Leganyer (1882–1939)'

Tipping, Marjorie J., 'Boyd, Theodore Penleigh (1890–1923)'

Thomas, David, 'McCubbin, Frederick (Fred) (1855–1917)'

Topliss, Helen, 'Roberts, Thomas William (Tom) (1856–1931)'

Williams, Fred, 'Bell, George Frederick Henry (1878–1966)'

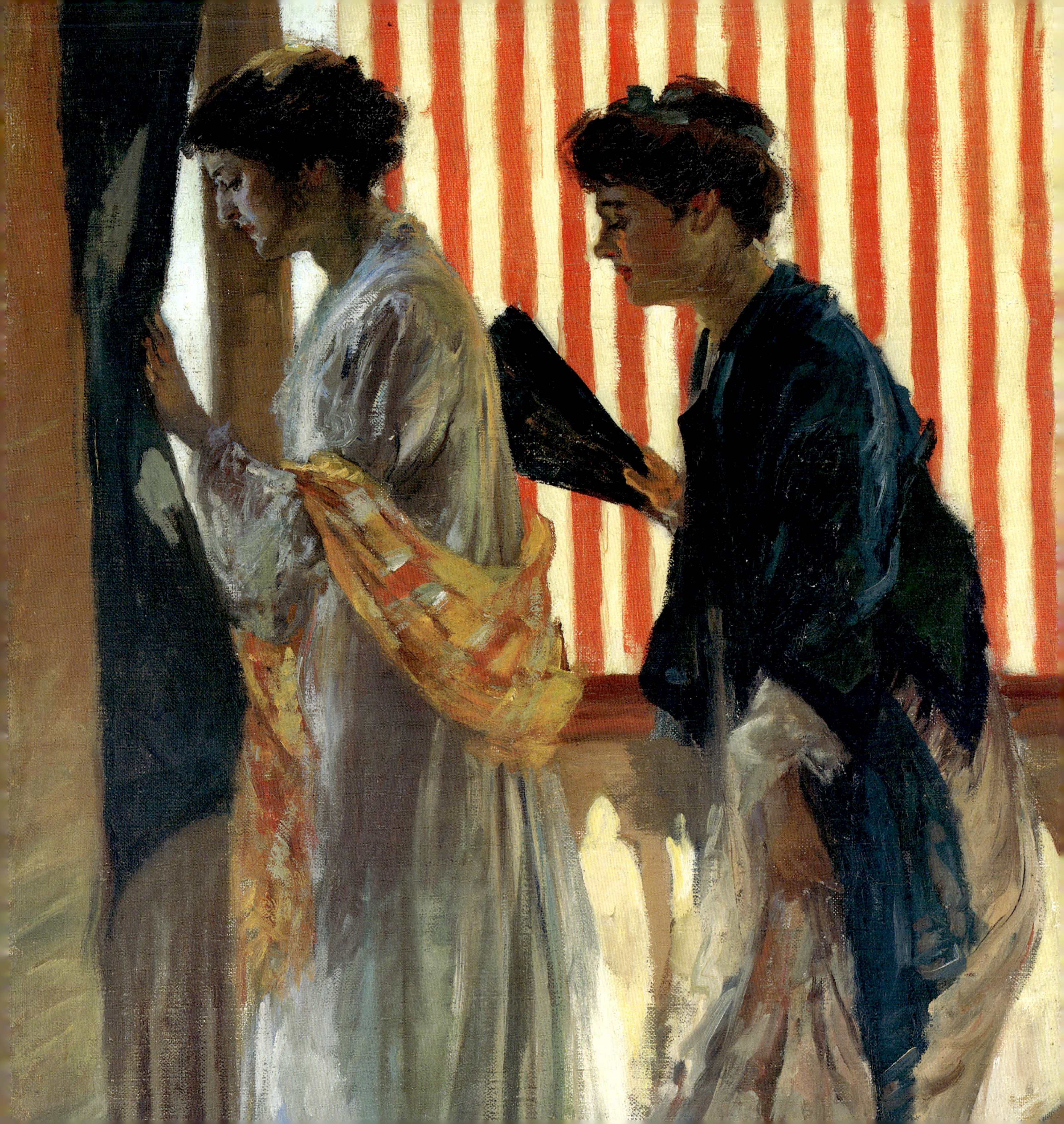

ACKNOWLEDGEMENTS

An exhibition and publication of this kind would not be possible without the professionalism, support and hard work of many National Gallery of Australia staff. *Capital and country: the Federation years 1900–1913* came into being due to the enthusiasm of the Gallery's Director Ron Radford, with the support of Anne Gray, Senior Curator of Australian Paintings and Sculpture before 1920. I thank them both for generously sharing their knowledge and passion for this period of Australian art history.

As the editor of this publication, Laura Murray Cree provided sound advice, professionalism and enthusiasm at every turn. I am also grateful to Simon Elliott, Assistant Director, Curatorial and Educational Services, and Deborah Hart, Senior Curator of Australian Paintings and Sculpture post-1920, who both generously gave their time and assistance throughout the course of this publication. I also extend my appreciation to curatorial colleagues Jacqueline Chlanda, Claire Capel-Stanley, Sarina Noordhuis-Fairfax and Emma Kindred.

Grateful thanks to Adam Worrall, Assistant Director, Exhibitions and Collections Services, Belinda Cotton, Head of Travelling Exhibitions and Georgia Connolly, the former Project Officer, Travelling Exhibitions, for the realisation of this exhibition and working with the venues around Australia. My gratitude to Bronwyn Campbell, Project Officer, Travelling Exhibitions, for preparing this exhibition for tour and for travelling with the show in the coming years.

To our dedicated Conservation team, sincere appreciation, especially Debbie Ward, David Wise, Sheridan Palmer, Sharon Alcock, Greg Howard, and Andrea Wise and her Paper Conservation team. Consultants John Jones and Rob Murdoch have carefully sourced and prepared appropriate replica period-frames for a number of key works in this exhibition.

To Kirsty Morrison, Head of Design for overseeing the publication, and to Kristin Thomas, Graphic Designer, thank you for weaving your magic with the layout of this catalogue, and to Carla Da Silva. My gratitude to Nick Nicholson for obtaining copyright permissions and supplementary images, and to the Imaging Services team, David Pang, Marcus Hayman, Lisa Mattiazzi, Eleni Krypidis, Alanna Bishop, John Tassie and Wilhelmina Kemperman for all in-house photography. Michelle Fracaro along with the Learning and Access team have developed exciting and thoughtful education material associated with this exhibition.

Many thanks also to the Exhibition Design team, especially Jing-Ling Chua, for the preparation of exhibition material. I am grateful to Registration staff Natalie Beattie, Mark Van Veen, Kate Buckingham and Jane Saker, as well as to Art Packers Tedd Nugent and Chris Harman, for their efforts to ensure that these paintings travel safely around the country.

My appreciation goes to the Gallery's Marketing and Communications staff, Shanthini Naidoo, Assistant Director Development, Marketing and Commercial Operations, and her talented team, David Edghill, Siobhan Ion, Jennifer Dobbins and Kate Groves, for helping people around Australia hear about the exhibition, and to Andrew Powrie and Julia Greenstreet for the exhibition's online presence.

I am grateful to the curatorial and registration staff of the Australian Parliament and the National Library of Australia for facilitating the loans to this exhibition.

Finally, to the supporters of the National Gallery of Australia Council Exhibitions Fund, Visions Australia and the National Collecting Institutions Touring and Outreach Program, thank you for your foresight in developing programs to facilitate sharing the national collections with all Australians.

Miriam Kelly

Produced by the Publishing Section,
National Gallery of Australia, Canberra

Photography by Imaging Services, National Gallery
of Australia unless otherwise credited

nga.gov.au

The National Gallery of Australia is an Australian
Government Agency

Publication coordinator: Simon Elliott
Edit: Laura Murray Cree
Design: Kristin Thomas
Rights and Permissions: Nick Nicholson
Index: Sherrey Quinn
Prepress: Splitting Image, Melbourne
Print: Australian Book Connection

National Library of Australia
Cataloguing-in-Publication entry
Author: Kelly, Miriam, author.
Title: Capital and country: the federation years
1900 – 1913 / Miriam Kelly.
ISBN: 9780642334398 (pbk.)
Notes: Includes bibliographical references and index.
Subjects: Painting — Australia — Exhibitions.
Dewey Number: 759.9940749471

Distributed in Australia by
NewSouth Books
45 Beach Street
Coogee NSW 2034 Australia

Distributed in the United States of America by
University of Washington Press
4333 Brooklyn Avenue NE
Seattle, WA 98195-9570

(cover) **W.C. Piguenit** (detail)
Near Liverpool, New South Wales c. 1908
National Gallery of Australia, Canberra, acquired with the assistance
of the Masterpieces for the Nation Fund 2005

(page 2) **Hans Heysen** (detail)
The saplings 1904
National Gallery of Australia, Canberra, bequest of Millie Hay Joyner 1993

(pages 4–5) **E. Phillips Fox** (detail)
Promenade c. 1909
National Gallery of Australia, Canberra, purchased 1974

(pages 6–7) **Penleigh Boyd** (detail)
The Federal Capital site 1913
Australian Parliament House, Canberra, Historic Memorials Collection,
purchased 1913

(page 8) **Harry Garlick** (detail)
The drover 1906
National Gallery of Australia, Canberra, purchased 1972

(pages 10-11) **W.C. Piguenit** (detail)
Near Liverpool, New South Wales c. 1908
National Gallery of Australia, Canberra, acquired with the assistance
of the Masterpieces for the Nation Fund 2005

(page 28–29) **Frederick McCubbin** (detail)
Flood waters 1913
National Gallery of Australia, Canberra, purchased 1973

(page 76–77) **George W. Lambert** (detail)
The sonnet c. 1907
National Gallery of Australia, Canberra, bequest of John B. Pye 1963

(page 122-123) **Richard Hayley-Lever** (detail)
A haven beneath the hill, St Ives c. 1908
National Gallery of Australia, Canberra, purchased 1968

(page 132-133) **Rupert Bunny** (detail)
Qui vient? [*Who comes?*] c. 1908
oil on canvas, 81 x 54.2 cm
National Gallery of Australia, Canberra, bequest of John B. Pye 1963

Image credits

pp. 2, 16, 40, 41, 82, 83, 84, 85 © Hans Heysen.
Licensed by Viscopy

pp.18, 48, 49 Reproduced with the kind permission
of the Ophthalmic Research Institute of Australia

pp. 102, 103 © Rix Wright

pp. 114, 115 © A. Niven

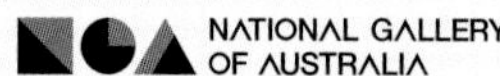

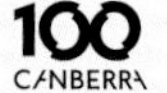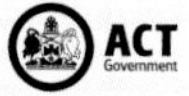

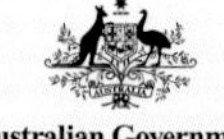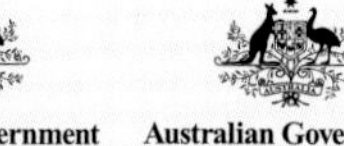

**National Gallery of Australia
Council Exhibitions Fund**

Supported by Visions of Australia, an Australian
Government Program supporting touring exhibitions
by providing funding assistance for the development
and touring of cultural material across Australia,
and the National Collecting Institutions Touring
and Outreach Program, an Australian Government
program aiming to improve access to the national
collections for all Australians.

Published in conjunction with the National
Gallery of Australia's exhibition *Capital and country:
the Federation years 1900–1913,* touring nationally
2013–2015 to celebrate Federation and the national
capital in the year of Canberra's Centenary.

Museum & Art Gallery of the Northern Territory,
Darwin NT,
4 May – 29 September 2013

Art Gallery of Ballarat, Ballarat VIC,
26 October 2013 – 19 January 2014

Tasmanian Museum & Art Gallery,
Hobart TAS,
14 March – 11 May 2014

Riddoch Art Gallery, Mt Gambier SA,
13 December 2014 – 22 February 2015

Newcastle Art Gallery, Newcastle NSW,
7 March – 31 May 2015

UQ Art Museum, St Lucia QLD,
25 July – 1 November 2015